# Microsoft
# Pocket
# Guide

## to
## Microsoft®
## Outlook® 2000

**Microsoft Office Application**

PUBLISHED BY
Microsoft Press
A Division of Microsoft Corporation
One Microsoft Way
Redmond, Washington 98052-6399

Library of Congress Cataloging-in-Publication Data
Nelson, Stephen L. , 1959-
    Microsoft Pocket Guide to Microsoft Outlook 2000 / Stephen L.
Nelson
        p. cm.
        Includes index.
        ISBN 1-57231-978-X
        1. Microsoft Outlook.   2. Time management--Computer programs.
    3. Personal information management--Computer programs.  I. Title.
    HD69.T54N455    1999
    005.369--dc21

                                                        98-44770
                                                             CIP

Printed and bound in the United States of America.

1  2  3  4  5 6 7 8  9   MLML    4 3 2  1  0 9

Distributed in Canada by ITP Nelson, a division of Thomson Canada Limited.

A CIP catalogue record for this book is available from the British Library.

Microsoft Press books are available through booksellers and distributors worldwide. For further information about international editions, contact your local Microsoft Corporation office or contact Microsoft Press International directly at fax (425) 936-7329. Visit our Web site at mspress.microsoft.com.

**Acquisitions Editor:** Susanne M. Forderer
**Project Editor:** Anne Taussig

Microsoft
**Pocket
Guide**
to
Microsoft®
**Outlook**®2000

Microsoft Office Application

Stephen L. Nelson          ***Microsoft**·Press*

*The* Microsoft Pocket Guide to Microsoft Outlook 2000 *is divided into five sections. These sections are designed to help you find the information you need quickly.*

# 1 Environment

Terms and ideas you'll want to know to get the most out of Microsoft Outlook. All the basic parts of Outlook are shown and explained. The emphasis here is on quick answers, but many topics are cross-referenced so that you can find out more if you want to.

*Diagrams* of key components, with quick definitions, cross-referenced to more complete information.

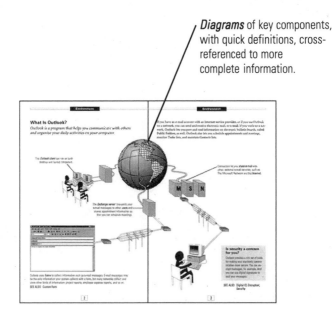

## Tips

Watch for these as you use this Pocket Guide. They'll point out helpful hints and let you know what to watch for.

# 15 Outlook A to Z

An alphabetic list of commands, tasks, terms, and procedures.

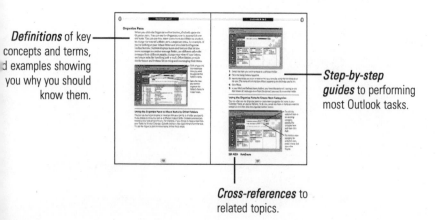

*Definitions* of key concepts and terms, and examples showing you why you should know them.

*Step-by-step guides* to performing most Outlook tasks.

*Cross-references* to related topics.

# 155 Troubleshooting

A guide to common problems—how to avoid them, and what to do when they occur.

# 165 Quick Reference

Useful indexes, including a full list of menu commands, shortcut keys, and more.

# 185 Index

A complete reference to all elements of the Pocket Guide.

# ntroduction

This Pocket Guide provides quick, practical answers to just about any question you have about Microsoft Outlook 2000. To acquaint yourself with this convenient and easy-to-use book, take two minutes now and read the Introduction. It explains how this unusual little book works.

# What Is a Pocket Guide?

One of the problems with the larger books about computers is, quite frankly, their size. With a large book, you must typically sift through pages of information to find that one piece of information you need. Not only that, you have to contend with their physical size. It's rarely enjoyable and often not practical to lug around a thousand-page book if you're working both at home and at the office, or if you're on the road with your laptop.

The *Microsoft Pocket Guide to Microsoft Outlook 2000* addresses both "size" problems of the larger computer books. Most obvious, of course, is the fact that this book is smaller. So it's easier to carry the book around wherever you go.

But this Pocket Guide also addresses the problem of wading through a large book to find the piece of information you need. And it does so in a variety of ways. For starters, this Pocket Guide organizes its information using an A to Z scheme—just like a dictionary or an encyclopedia does. This Pocket Guide supplies visual indexes in its Environment section, so you can find help even if you don't know how to describe what it is you're looking for. Finally, this Pocket Guide also uses a rich cross-referencing scheme that points you to related topics.

For new users, the Pocket Guide provides the essential information necessary to start using Outlook. And for experienced users, the Pocket Guide provides concise, easy-to-find descriptions of Outlook tasks, terms, and techniques.

# When You Have a Question

Let me explain how to find the information you need. If Outlook is new to you, flip first to the Environment section, which is a visual index. Find the picture that shows what you want to do or the task you have a question about. If you want to know how to send an e-mail message, for example, flip to pages 4 and 5, which talk about how you send an e-mail message over a network using Outlook.

Next read the captions that describe the parts of the picture. Say, for example, that you want to attach a file to send along with your message. On page 4 there's a caption that describes what message attachments are.

You'll notice that some captions use **boldface** terms or are followed by boldface terms. These refer to entries in the second section, Outlook A to Z, and provide more information related to the caption's contents.

Outlook A to Z is a dictionary of more than 200 entries that define terms and describe tasks. (After you've worked with Outlook a little or if you're already an experienced user, you'll often be able to turn directly to that section.) So if you have just read the caption in the Environment section that talks about message attachments, you'll see the term **item** in boldface, indicating a cross-reference. If you don't know what an Outlook item is, you can flip to the Items entry in Outlook A to Z.

When an entry in Outlook A to Z appears as a term within another entry, I'll often **boldface** it the first time it appears in that entry. For example, as part of describing what an Outlook item is, I might tell you that an appointment is an example of an Outlook item. In this case, the word **appointment** appears in bold letters—alerting you to the presence of another entry explaining appointments and how you create them using Outlook's Calendar. If you don't understand the term or want to do some brushing up, you can flip to the entry for more information.

# When You Have a Problem

The third section, Troubleshooting, describes problems that new or casual users of Outlook often encounter. Following each problem description, I list one or more solutions that you can employ to fix the problem.

# When You Wonder About a Command

The Quick Reference at the end of the Pocket Guide describes the menu commands and the toolbar buttons. If you want to know what a specific command or toolbar button does, turn to the Quick Reference. Don't forget about the index either. You can look there to find all references to any single topic in this book.

# Conventions Used Here

I have developed a few conventions to make using this book easier for you. Rather than use wordy phrases such as "Activate the File menu and then choose the Print command" to describe how you choose a menu command, I'm just going to say, "Choose the File menu's Print command."

Here's another convention: To make dialog box button and box labels stand out, I've capitalized the initial letter of each word in the label. I think this makes it easier to understand an instruction such as "Select the Print To File check box." With this scheme, it's easier to see, for example, that "Print To File" is a label.

Finally, I want to let you know about a couple of conventions I used when creating the figures for this book so that you won't get confused if the figures you see here look a little different than what you see on your screen. When I installed Outlook to create the figures for this book, I didn't upgrade from Outlook 97. This is why my Outlook Bar's buttons are called Outlook Shortcuts, My Shortcuts, and Other Shortcuts. If you upgraded from Outlook 97, your buttons may be called Outlook, Mail, and Other. But you have pretty much the same icons in each group as I do. The computer I used for creating the figures for this book is also part of a network. So I installed the Corporate or Workgroup version of Outlook. If you installed the Internet Only or No E-Mail version of Outlook, your Address Book might look a little different and you will have fewer options in some dialog boxes. Finally, I performed the full installation of Outlook so that I could tell you about some of the features in that version. If you installed the Standard or Minimal version, you might not have all of the features I talk about.

# Environment

Need to get oriented
quickly? Then the
Environment is the place
to start. It defines the key
terms you'll need to know
and the core ideas you
should understand as
you begin using
Microsoft Outlook 2000.

# What Is Outlook?

*Outlook is a program that helps you communicate with others and organize your daily activities on your computer.*

The *Outlook client* can run on both desktop and laptop computers.

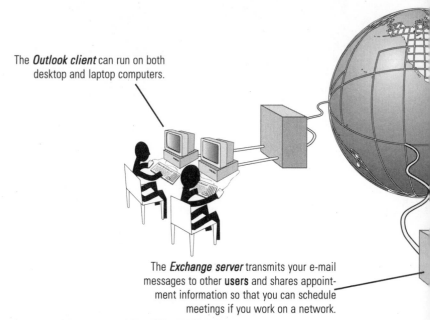

The *Exchange server* transmits your e-mail messages to other **users** and shares appointment information so that you can schedule meetings if you work on a network.

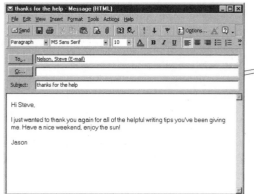

Outlook uses *forms* to collect information such as e-mail messages and contact information. You may only use the forms built into Outlook, but many networks collect and store other kinds of information using **custom forms**: project reports, employee expense reports, and so on.

If you have an e-mail account with an **Internet service provider,** or if you use Outlook on a **network,** you can send and receive electronic mail, or **e-mail.** If you work on a network, Outlook lets you **post** and read information on electronic bulletin boards, called **Public Folders,** as well. Outlook also lets you schedule **appointments** and meetings, monitor **Tasks** lists, and maintain **Contacts** lists.

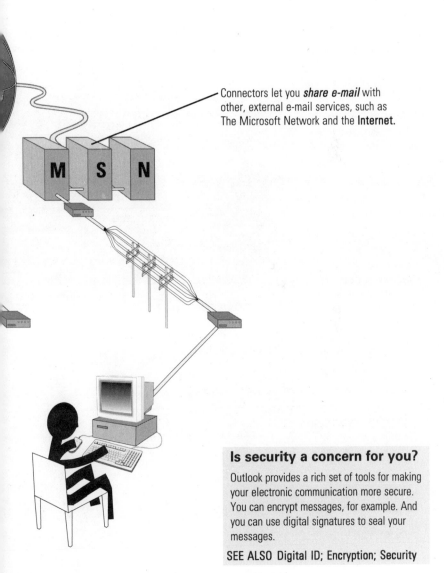

Connectors let you *share e-mail* with other, external e-mail services, such as The Microsoft Network and the **Internet.**

### Is security a concern for you?

Outlook provides a rich set of tools for making your electronic communication more secure. You can encrypt messages, for example. And you can use digital signatures to seal your messages.

SEE ALSO Digital ID; Encryption; Security

## Sending Your Messages

*With Outlook, you can easily send e-mail over the Internet, mail messages to network users, or send a fax using your fax/modem.*

*Send your message* by clicking the Send toolbar button when you finish the message.

Click To or Cc to see the *Address Book.* It lists the names of everyone in your organization so that you can easily find and use their addresses to send messages.
**SEE ALSO Blind Carbon Copy; Copy; Distribution List; E-Mail Name**

Type the *message body* into the main part of the Message form.

*Message attachments* let you send a file or another Outlook **item** with your message.

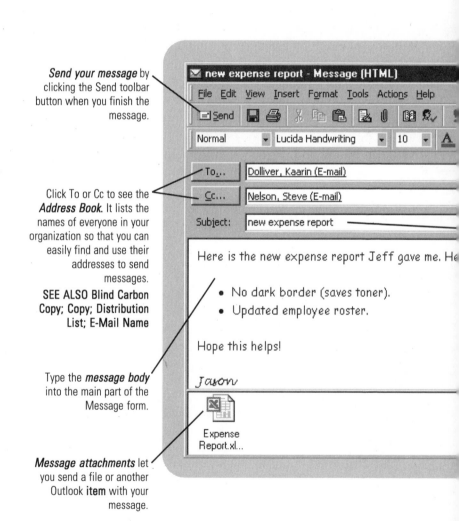

4

To create a **message,** you use the **Message form** to name the **recipient,** identify the message **subject,** and then type the body of your message. While text-only messages are probably most common, you can also use Outlook to embed images in your messages and attach **files.**

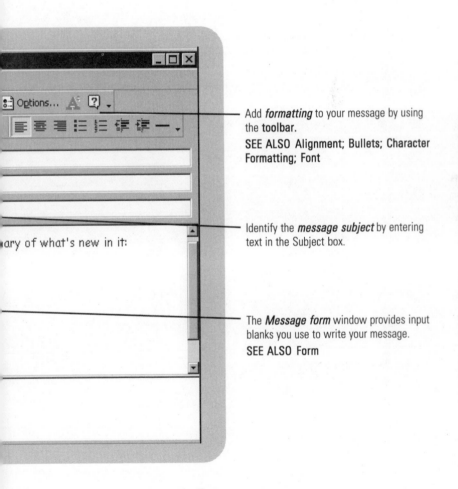

Add *formatting* to your message by using the **toolbar.**
SEE ALSO Alignment; Bullets; Character Formatting; Font

Identify the *message subject* by entering text in the Subject box.

The *Message form* window provides input blanks you use to write your message.
SEE ALSO Form

# Reading Your Messages

*Outlook makes it easy to organize and read your incoming messages. The Inbox is Outlook's incoming message center.*

The *Folder List* displays your Personal Folders and any folders you have open. Click the **Inbox** folder to view incoming messages.

Click one of the icons on the *Outlook Bar* to move to that **folder** or location.

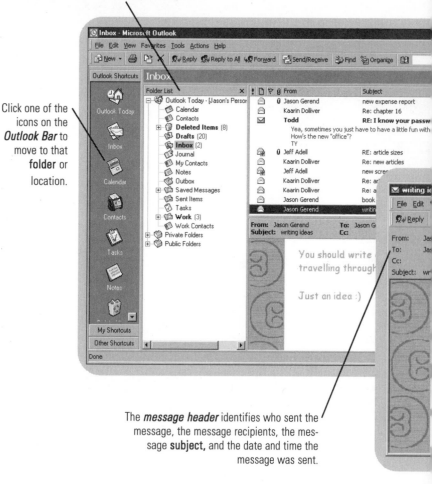

The *message header* identifies who sent the message, the message recipients, the message **subject,** and the date and time the message was sent.

Outlook uses **folders** to organize items. **Personal Folders** store the messages you receive, your contacts, and all of your other Outlook items. **Web Folders** store web pages and **iCalendar** information you post to your web site, while **Public Folders** store the **posts** that you want to make available to other **users** on a network. When you find the folder with the item you want to view, double-click the item to open it.

The *information viewer* shows the messages in a folder grouped and sorted any way you want. Select a message to view it in the Preview pane; double-click a message to open it.
SEE ALSO Grouping Items; Preview Pane; Read and Unread Messages; Sorting

When you open a *message* it appears in its own window so you can read it easily. The Message window also provides **toolbar** buttons that you can use to print, delete, **reply** to, or **forward** the message.

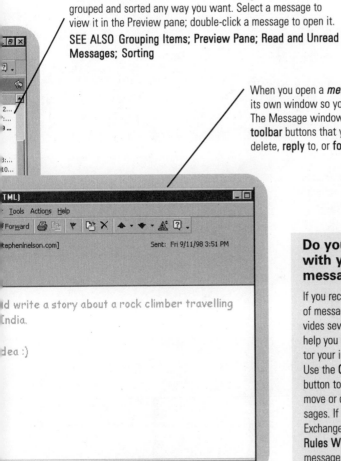

## Do you need help with your messages?

If you receive a large number of messages, Outlook provides several useful tools to help you manage and monitor your incoming messages. Use the **Organize** toolbar button to automatically move or color your messages. If you use Microsoft Exchange services, the **Rules Wizard** alerts you to messages you receive and can also reply to and forward messages. The **Out Of Office Assistant** automatically replies to messages when you're away from your computer.

# How the Calendar Works

*Outlook helps you maintain an appointment calendar and a task list.*

You can tell Outlook to display *Reminders* that alert you to upcoming appointments and **events.**

Click one of the icons on the **Outlook Bar** to move to that **folder** or location.

*Appointments* are entered in time-slots in your Calendar.
**SEE ALSO Private Appointments and Tasks; Recurring Appointment**

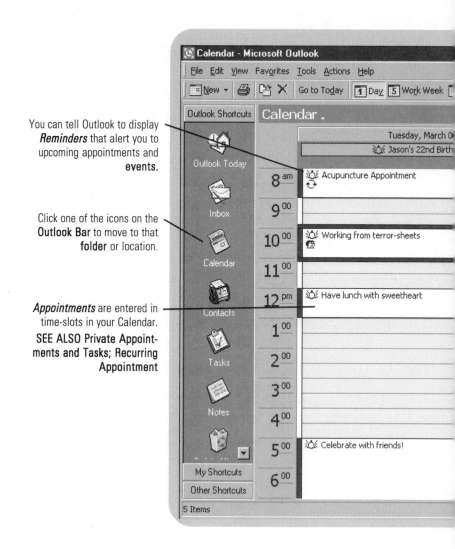

You use the **Calendar** to schedule your time commitments: meetings, **appointments**, deadlines, and so forth. You use the **TaskPad** to keep track of the **tasks** you need to complete.

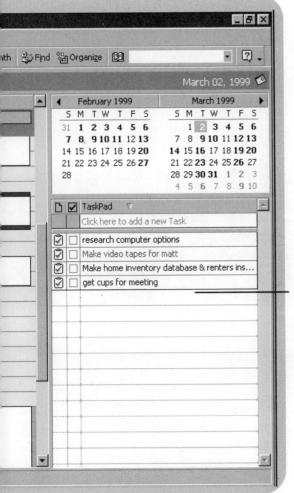

Meetings are easy to schedule because Outlook does the work of finding the earliest open time-slot that the meeting attendees have in common.

SEE ALSO Busy Time; Delegate Access; Permission

The *TaskPad* is a compact version of the Tasks list that lets you keep track of the individual tasks that you need to complete.

SEE ALSO Recurring Task

# Keeping Track of Your Contacts

*The Contacts folder lets you keep records of business and personal contacts.*

Click one of the icons on the **Outlook Bar** to move to that **folder** or location.

Double-click an address card to display complete information about a **contact**.
**SEE ALSO Address Book; Views**

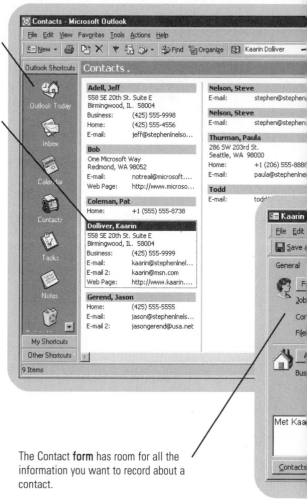

The Contact **form** has room for all the information you want to record about a contact.

You can use the **Contacts** list to keep track of the names, mailing addresses, phone numbers, and e-mail addresses of all your customers, vendors, contractors, friends, family members, and acquaintances. You can display and view information about your contacts in a list or as alphabetized index cards.

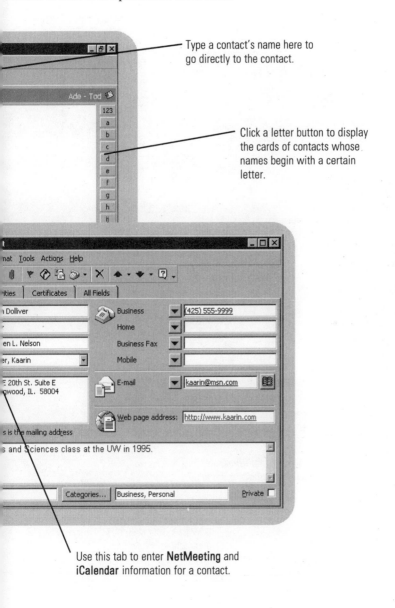

Type a contact's name here to go directly to the contact.

Click a letter button to display the cards of contacts whose names begin with a certain letter.

Use this tab to enter **NetMeeting** and **iCalendar** information for a contact.

11

# Keeping a Journal and Writing Notes

*The Journal folder lets you automatically track messages, tasks, and even Microsoft Office files. Notes are handy ways to post reminders.*

Click one of the icons on the **Outlook Bar** to move to that **folder** or location.

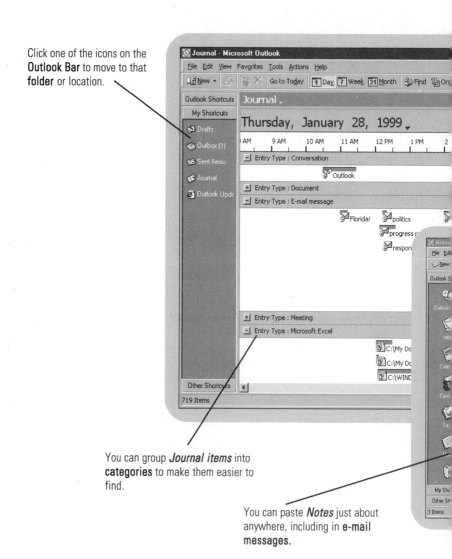

You can group *Journal items* into **categories** to make them easier to find.

You can paste *Notes* just about anywhere, including in **e-mail messages**.

12

Use the **Journal** to automatically maintain a running list of all the messages you send and receive, notes you write, tasks you work on, and Microsoft **Word,** Microsoft Excel, and Microsoft PowerPoint files you create. Or add manual Journal entries for activities you do away from your computer—for letters you write or projects you work on. View your Journal events against a timeline or in a list. Create **Notes** to paste on your desktop or in messages, and color-code them for easy filing.

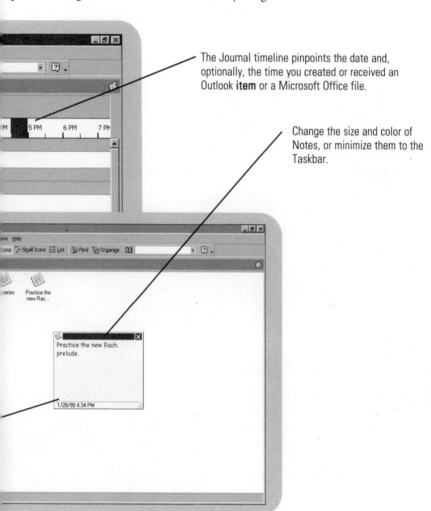

The Journal timeline pinpoints the date and, optionally, the time you created or received an Outlook **item** or a Microsoft Office file.

Change the size and color of Notes, or minimize them to the Taskbar.

# Outlook

## A to Z

When you have a question, you want a quick, easy answer. Outlook A to Z, which starts on the next page, should provide just these sorts of answers. It lists in alphabetic order the tools, terms, and techniques you'll need to know.

## Actions

Within Outlook, the term *action* can refer to two separate things. *Actions* is the name of a menu with unique commands for working with a folder's items. For example, when the **Inbox** is displayed, the Actions menu provides commands for working with messages. And when the **Tasks** folder is displayed, the Actions menu provides commands for working with tasks. (By the way, because the **Outlook folders** offer such similar menus, once you learn how to work with one folder, you'll find it very easy to work with the others.)

The term *actions* also refers to automatic responses that you tell Outlook to perform in certain situations. For example, you can tell Outlook to open the next **message** in the **Inbox information viewer** after you delete the current message. You can set controls for most actions on the various tabs of the Options dialog box, which you open by choosing the Tools menu's Options command.

**SEE ALSO    Rules Wizard; Quick Reference: Actions Menu Commands**

## Activities

Outlook automatically keeps track of all interactions with a contact and displays them for you in the contact's **Contact Item** window on the Activities tab. Here you can view all information recorded by the **Journal,** such as e-mail messages and manually recorded phone calls, as well as any active appointments or tasks. Clicking the Activities tab is a quick way to see everything Outlook knows about your interactions with a particular contact.

**SEE ALSO    Contacts; Journal**

## Adaptability

Outlook customizes its menus so that they supply only the commands you choose and its toolbars so that they provide only the tools you use. This adaptability makes it easier for you to find the menu commands and toolbar buttons you regularly use.

You still have access to all of Outlook's features even with its adaptability, however. If you point to the double arrow at the bottom of a menu or linger on a menu or open several menus without choosing a command, Outlook displays its long menus, which supply all your commands. If you click the double arrow toolbar button, you display an extended set of toolbar buttons.

**SEE ALSO    Troubleshooting: You Can't Find a Menu Command or Toolbar Button**

## Address Book

Outlook provides a tool called the Address Book that you can use to find the name and address information you need to send e-mail. The Address Book lists all the people you've described using the **Contacts** folder, all the people that appear on the **Global Address List** (if your computer is connected to a network that includes Microsoft **Exchange Server**), and all the people you've described using a **Personal Address Book.** In some cases, the Address Book even provides access to other lists of e-mail addresses, too.

### Adding E-Mail Names to an Address Book List

If you have already received a **message** from someone, it's easy to add this person's name to your Contacts folder or to your Personal Address Book for easy reference in the future. Just open the message that the person sent you, and then right-click the sender's name in the message header. To add the sender's name and address to your Contacts folder, choose the shortcut menu's Add To Contacts command and enter information about the sender. If you have specified that personal addresses should be stored in your Personal Address Book and you want to add an address to it, choose the shortcut menu's Add To Personal Address Book command. To change the way Outlook prioritizes your address lists, choose the Tools menu's Address Book command. In the Address Book window, choose the Tools menu's Options command. Choose the options you want, and then click OK.

If you want to add the e-mail address and name of someone from whom you haven't received a message to your Address Book, you can add a contact to the Contacts folder by displaying the Contacts folder and clicking the New Contact button. If you're not using the Contacts folder and are instead using a Personal Address Book, you can use the Address Book to add an e-mail name and address. To do this, click the Address Book toolbar button to display the Address Book and click the New Entry toolbar button to add a new entry to an Address Book list. Then select the type of entry you want to add and the Address Book list to which you want to add it. Enter the person's address using the various tabs of the dialog box that Outlook provides.

*continues*

## Address Book *(continued)*

### Using Address Book Names to Send E-Mail

Typically, you use the information in the Address Book to e-mail someone a message. To do this, click To or Cc on the Message form. Outlook displays the Select Names dialog box.

Click the down arrow in the Show Names From The drop-down list to specify whether you want to see the names of people in your Contacts folder or on some other list such as the Global Address List or your Personal Address Book. Then to select someone in the Address Book, double-click a name to add it to the Message Recipients list.

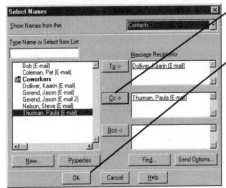

Click Cc to send a copy of the message to someone.

After the names of everyone who should receive the message have been added to the Message Recipients list, click OK.

**SEE ALSO    Contacts; Distribution List**

## Alignment

You can change the alignment of a paragraph or paragraphs in the Message form as long as you're sending a **Rich Text** or **HTML** message. To do this, simply click the paragraph you want to align (or to align several paragraphs at once, click in one and drag over the others) and then click the Align Left, Center, or Align Right toolbar buttons.

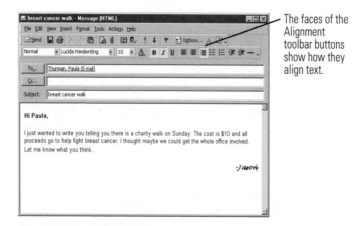

The faces of the Alignment toolbar buttons show how they align text.

## Annual Event SEE Event

## Appointment

Outlook lets you record appointments in the **Calendar.** To add an appointment, click the Calendar icon on the **Outlook Bar.** Then click the appointment date on the **Date Navigator.**

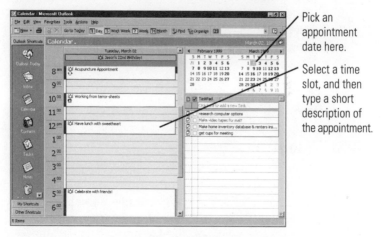

Pick an appointment date here.

Select a time slot, and then type a short description of the appointment.

Alternatively, to provide more detailed information about an appointment you're adding, just double-click any block of time. Or click the New Appointment toolbar button. Then use the Appointment dialog box to describe the appointment in detail.

*continues*

19

## Appointment *(continued)*

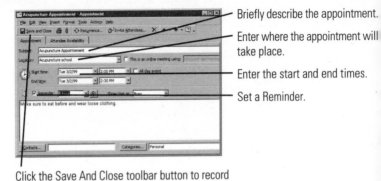

Briefly describe the appointment.

Enter where the appointment will take place.

Enter the start and end times.

Set a Reminder.

Click the Save And Close toolbar button to record the appointment.

**SEE ALSO    Recurring Appointment**

---

## Archive SEE **AutoArchive**

---

## Attachment

The term *attachment* refers to a **file** or Outlook item you attach to another Outlook item. For example, you can attach a Microsoft Office document you're working on to a task. Or you can attach a task item to an appointment. But you probably most commonly want to attach files to e-mail **messages** or **posts**. This is a quick and convenient way of sharing documents with other people.

**SEE ALSO    MIME; Uuencode**

---

## AutoArchive

Outlook allows you to create archives. An archive is a portion of an existing **Outlook folder** that is stored in a separate file, which is called an archive. For example, suppose you had two years' worth of scheduling information, for 1998 and 1999, in an existing file. You could create an archive for the 1998 scheduling information. This way, the information no longer appears in your regular schedule— and Outlook runs faster—although the information remains available in the archive in case you ever need it.

Outlook will automatically archive items in the **Calendar, Inbox, Journal,** and Sent Items folders. What's more, you can tell Outlook to archive items in other Outlook folders, or you can turn off AutoArchive altogether. (You can't archive items in the **Contacts** folder because contact items usually don't become obsolete just because they're old.) You can also tell AutoArchive to delete old items instead of archiving them.

### Setting AutoArchive Options

To set AutoArchive options, choose the Tools menu's Options command, click the Other tab, and then click AutoArchive.

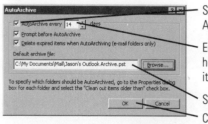

Select this check box to turn on AutoArchive.

Enter a number in this box to specify how often Outlook should archive old items.

Specify the archive file here.

Click OK.

### Setting AutoArchive Folder Options

You set AutoArchive options individually for each folder you want to archive. To set options for the **Sent Items** folder, for example, click the My Shortcuts group on the Outlook Bar, and then right-click the Sent Items icon and choose the shortcut menu's Properties command. When Outlook displays the Sent Items Properties dialog box, click the AutoArchive tab.

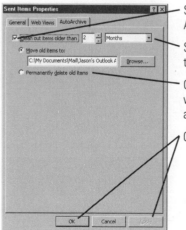

Select this check box to turn on AutoArchive for this folder.

Specify the age of items to archive with these boxes.

Click one of these option buttons to specify whether to archive or delete items that are older than the date you set.

Click Apply, and then click OK.

*continues*

## AutoArchive *(continued)*

### Creating Archives Manually

To create Outlook archives manually, choose the File menu's Archive command. When Outlook displays the Archive dialog box, name the archive file, specify where you want the file stored, and enter a cutoff date.

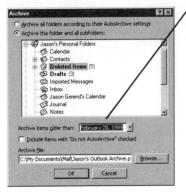

Items older than this date go into the archive file; everything else stays with the original file.

---

### Retrieving Archives

To retrieve the items stored in an archive file, follow these steps:

**1** Choose the File menu's Open command, and then choose the submenu's Personal Folder File (.pst) command.

**2** Use the Look In drop-down list box to find the folder storing your archive. (The default filename and path is C:\WINDOWS\ApplicationData\Microsoft\Outlook\archive.pst.)

**3** Click OK to open the file.

**4** Use the **Folder view** to open the different folders in your archive. When you find an item you want to move back to your **Personal Folder File,** click and drag it to the folder you want to store the item in.

**5** When you're finished, right-click Archive Folders in the Folder List, and then choose the shortcut menu's Close "Archive Folders" command to close your archives.

# AutoCreate

Outlook lets you automatically create new **items** by dragging an item from one folder to another. For example, if you drag a meeting request from your Inbox to the Calendar folder or a task request from your Inbox to the Tasks folder, Outlook automatically creates new calendar and task items. (In these two special cases, Outlook also sends an acceptance reply to the sender.)

**SEE ALSO    Plan A Meeting Wizard**

# AutoDial

If you have a modem and a phone on the same line, Outlook can dial the phone for you. In the **Contacts** folder, click the contact you want to call, and click the AutoDialer toolbar button. Outlook displays the New Call dialog box for the selected contact.

*continues*

## AutoDial *(continued)*

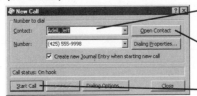

Outlook displays the name of the selected contact here.

Click here to display all the phone numbers you've recorded for this contact.

Click here to initiate the call.

**SEE ALSO** **Speed Dial**

## Automatic Delivery

If your computer connects to a network that includes an **Exchange server,** Outlook automatically delivers your messages. When you click the Send toolbar button in the **Message form,** the Outlook client immediately sends the message to the Exchange server. Shortly thereafter, the Exchange server sends the message to the recipient's Outlook client. Depending on how the administrator set up the server and the client, sending messages can take a few seconds or a few minutes. If your messages aren't being delivered quickly, something is amiss. You need to have a little chat with the administrator.

**SEE ALSO** **Deferred Delivery**

## AutoPreview

You can preview the first few lines of new messages in your **Inbox** information viewer without actually displaying the messages themselves. To do this, choose the View menu's AutoPreview command.

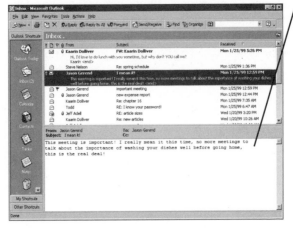

Messages appear like this when the AutoPreview view is used.

You can preview tasks in your Tasks list, too.

### Previewing All Messages

You can also preview all your messages by choosing the View menu's Current View command and the submenu's Customize Current View command. Then click Other Settings, select Preview All Items in the AutoPreview section of the Other Settings dialog box, and click OK when finished. Click OK to return to Outlook.

**SEE ALSO    Preview Pane**

## AutoReply SEE Out Of Office Assistant

## Blind Carbon Copy

A blind carbon copy is a **copy** of a **message** sent to one **recipient** without the recipient's name appearing on the copies sent to the other recipients. However, the recipients' names do appear in the message **header**, which is something relatively easy to view.

To send blind carbon copies, display the **Message form** and then choose the View menu's Bcc Field command. Use the Bcc box to name the recipients to whom you want to send a blind carbon copy of a message.

When you choose the View menu's Bcc Field command, Outlook adds the Bcc box to the Message form.

## Body SEE Message Body

## Bullets

Outlook lets you include bullets in e-mail messages formatted either in **HTML** or **Rich Text** format. To create a bulleted list, selec the paragraphs that you want to turn into a bulleted list and click the Bullets toolbar button. Note as well that you can also create numbered lists in **HTML messages** using the Numbering toolbar button.

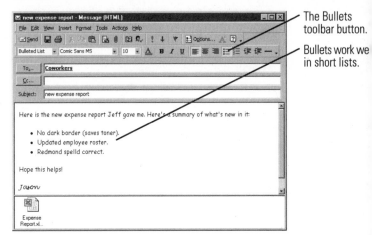

The Bullets toolbar button.

Bullets work we in short lists.

### Bullets are a paragraph formatting option

When you click the Bullets toolbar button, Outlook doesn't add a bullet to the beginning of each line but to the beginning of each paragraph you selected. To start each line with a bullet, you need to create short, one-line paragraphs by pressing the Enter key at the end of each line.

## Busy Time

Outlook calls the time slots that you've already filled with **appointments** your *busy times*. You can see your busy times blocked out on the **Calendar.** The opposite of busy time is free time, by the way.

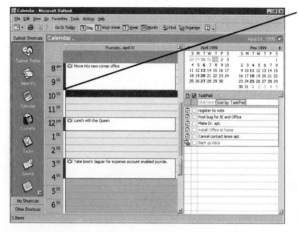

Onscreen, the busy times appear in blue.

## Calendar

The Calendar is an **Outlook folder** that lets you schedule **appointments,** meetings, or any of the ordinary activities and **events** that seem to fill up everyone's days. Your dentist appointment. The kids' birthdays. Your anniversary. You get the idea.

If you've used Microsoft **Schedule+**, the Calendar will look pretty familiar to you. (Incidentally, if you're a former Schedule+ user, you can import your old schedule into Outlook. See the entry on the **Import And Export** command.)

The Calendar folder has several components.

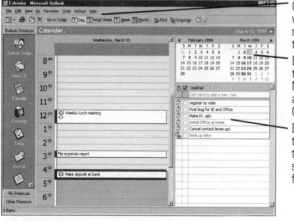

Choose daily, weekly, or monthly views in the Calendar.

Dates selected in the Date Navigator appear on the Calendar.

Drag a task from the TaskPad onto the Calendar to schedule a time for the task.

*continues*

## Calendar *(continued)*

### Changing the Calendar View

Outlook lets you view your Calendar information in a variety of ways. Accordingly, you will probably want to experiment with the Calendar on your own to find the views that work best for you.

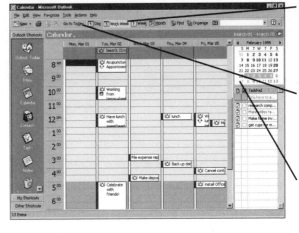

**1** Click these toolbar buttons to view different amounts of time.

**2** Click the Go To Today toolbar button to view today's schedule.

**3** Click in the Date Navigator to move around in the Calendar.

## Customizing the Calendar view

You can also customize the view of your Calendar. This works the same way as it does for Outlook's other folders. Just choose the View menu's Current View command and the submenu's Customize Current View command. In the View Summary dialog box, you can change the way appointments and events are filtered. You can also change the amount of information displayed in the Calendar by adding or removing **fields** from the view. And depending on the view you have displayed, you can change the way Outlook sorts and groups appointments and events in lists.

### Setting Calendar Display Options

You can set various Calendar display options, including establishing the work week and designating working hours, by using the Calendar Options dialog box. To display the Calendar Options dialog box, choose the Tools menu's Options command, click the Preferences tab, and then click Calendar Options.

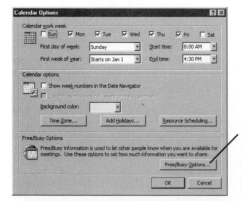

Click Free/Busy Options to set options for publishing your free and busy time to an Exchange server or to the Internet using the iCalendar format.

### Adding Birthdays and Anniversaries to the Calendar

In Outlook, activities or occasions that last a full day or more are called events. Events include occasions such as conventions, trade shows, or birthdays. Events differ from appointments in that they don't occupy time in your schedule. To show that events occur but don't take time, Outlook records events by simply placing a notice, or banner, on the Calendar. To add an annual event such as a birthday or anniversary to your Calendar, follow these steps:

1 Click the Calendar icon on the Outlook Bar.

2 Choose the Actions menu's New All Day Event command. Outlook displays the Event form.

3 Click the Recurrence toolbar button.

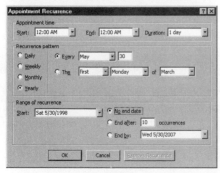

4 Under Recurrence Pattern, click the Yearly option button and enter the date of the birthday or anniversary. Click OK. Outlook redisplays the Untitled—Recurring Event form.

5 In the Subject box, name the birthday or anniversary.

*continues*

## Calendar *(continued)*

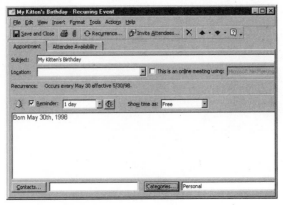

**6** Set a **Reminder** if you need time to prepare for an event. (In the case of a birthday, for example, you might want time to send a card or buy a gift.)

**7** Type any notes or comments.

**8** Optionally, click Contacts to associate the event with a contact or Categories to categorize the event.

**9** Click the Save And Close toolbar button.

---

### Adding Holidays to the Calendar

Outlook knows the names and dates of the official holidays in many of the world's countries and for several religions. To add holidays to your Calendar, follow these steps:

**1** Choose the Tools menu's Options command. Outlook displays the Options dialog box.

**2** Click the Preferences tab.

**3** Click Calendar Options. Outlook displays the Calendar Options dialog box.

**4** Click Add Holidays. Outlook displays the Add Holidays To Calendar dialog box.

**5** Select the holiday sets you want to add from the list box, and then click OK.

**6** Click OK again in the Calendar Options dialog box. Outlook adds the holidays to your Calendar.

## Using the Calendar to schedule appointments and meetings

To quickly block out time for appointments or meetings, display the daily Calendar for the day on which you want to schedule the appointment or meeting. Select the block of time the appointment or meeting will occupy. Right-click the selected block of time, and choose an appointment or meeting command from the shortcut menu. Outlook displays the appropriate form and enters the starting and ending times for you. Fill out the rest of the form, click the Save And Close toolbar button, and you're finished.

### Publishing Your Free/Busy Information

You can publish the times when you are free and busy to either an Exchange server or to the Internet by using the iCalendar standard. Your Exchange server Free/Busy information is set up and updated automatically; to set up Outlook to publish to the Internet, follow these steps or consult your **Internet service provider** for instructions:

**1** Choose the Tools menu's Options command, click the Preferences tab, and then click Calendar Options.

**2** Click Free/Busy Options, select the Publish My Free/Busy Information check box, and then enter the location of your web site and a filename ending with .vfb in the Publish At This URL text box. Click OK.

To update your Free/Busy information on the Internet, choose the Tools menu's Send And Receive command and then choose the submenu's Free/Busy Information command.

### Publishing Your Calendar as a Web Page

You can save a copy of your Calendar to your web site as an HTML page. To do this, choose the File menu's Save As Web Page command. Choose the start and end dates to be published, name the calendar, and click the Browse button. Click the **Web Folders** shortcut, select your web site from the list of web servers you set up, and then click OK. Click Save to connect to the Internet, and upload your Calendar to your web site.

**SEE ALSO**   **Net Folders; Plan A Meeting Wizard; Second Time Zone**

# Categories

You can assign Outlook **items** to various categories to make them easier to **sort, group,** and **find.** Outlook has 20 built-in categories, including business, personal, ideas, and miscellaneous. And it's easy to create new categories as you need them.

*continues*

## Categories *(continued)*

### Assigning an Item to a Category

To assign an item to a category, follow these steps:

**1** Right-click the item in the information viewer.

**2** Choose the shortcut menu's Categories command. Outlook displays the Categories dialog box.

**3** Select one of the existing categories in the Available Categories list, and click OK.

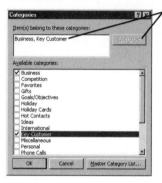

Type a new category name in this box, and then click Add To List.

## Using categories to group tasks into projects

Outlook doesn't automatically group tasks into projects, but that needn't stop you from using Outlook for basic project management. Just create a category for each project you start. For example, you might create a category called "Renovating the bathroom" or "Fall marketing campaign." Thereafter, every time you add a new task associated with the bathroom renovation project or the marketing campaign, you assign it to one of the new categories. Then you can group tasks by category to collect all the project tasks under the same heading.

## Cc SEE Copy

## Character Formatting

You can format characters in **messages.** Probably the easiest way to do it is by using the Formatting **toolbar** along the top of the **Message form.** The following figure points out the location of the Formatting toolbar. To format a bit of text, select the text and then click a Formatting toolbar button or select an entry in a Formatting toolbar drop-down list box. Before you add character formatting to messages, however, keep in mind that depending on the e-mail client the message recipient has, they may not be able to see the formatting you apply. So don't rely on formatting to carry your message's message.

This is the Formatting toolbar.

**SEE ALSO    Alignment**

## Check Names

You can verify that you typed the names of message **recipients** correctly. To do this, click the Check Names toolbar button in the **Message form** window.

You don't have to type someone's entire name when you address an e-mail message, however—only enough of the name for Outlook to identify the recipient. When Kaarin sends a message addressed to "Stephen N" on our little **network,** for example, it gets to me even though the **Global Address List** shows my name as "Stephen Nelson." And I can send a message back to "Kaarin" or even just "Kaa" even though the Global Address List shows her name as "Kaarin Dolliver." When you click Check Names, Outlook replaces the partial name you entered with the full user name—provided it can match the partial name to a name in one of the address lists in the **Address Book.** (If Outlook can't figure out to whom you want to send a message, it asks you for more information about the recipient.)

**SEE ALSO    Spelling Checker**

## Connection Wizard

Microsoft **Internet Explorer** comes with a Connection Wizard that you can use to set up a new Dial-Up Networking connection even after you initially set up Outlook and Internet Explorer. To use the Connection Wizard, click the Start button and then choose Programs, Internet Explorer, and Connection Wizard. By following the onscreen instructions, the wizard does everything necessary to connect your computer to the Internet. Once you run the wizard, you should be able to browse the **World Wide Web,** send and receive **e-mail,** and view newsgroups.

**SEE ALSO    Newsreader**

## Contacts

The Contacts folder provides you with an electronic phone and address book for tracking nearly every conceivable kind of information about your friends, family, and associates.

You enter contact information in the New Contact **form.** And you can even include their **e-mail** and **web page** addresses.

Like the other **Outlook folders,** Contacts can be viewed in several different ways. Address Cards is a particularly useful **view**—it's like an electronic Rolodex file with a built-in index.

### Adding a Contact to the Contacts List

To add a new contact to the Contacts list, either click the New Contact toolbar button or choose the File menu's New command and the submenu's Contact command. Outlook displays the Untitled—Contact form. Enter the contact's name, mailing address, phone numbers, and so forth in the text boxes provided, and click the Save And Close toolbar button when you're finished.

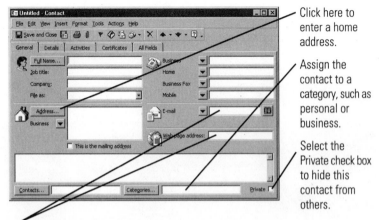

Click here to enter a home address.

Assign the contact to a category, such as personal or business.

Select the Private check box to hide this contact from others.

Enter the contact's e-mail and web page addresses in these boxes.

### Changing the View of the Contacts List

To change the view of the Contacts list, follow these steps:

**1** First display it by clicking the Contacts icon on the Outlook Bar.

**2** Choose the View menu's Current View command.

**3** Choose a view from the submenu, or choose the Customize Current View command or the Define Views command. Choose the Customize Current View command to add or rearrange the fields in the current view or to change the way Outlook groups, sorts, and filters contacts in the current view. Choose the Define Views command to add a view of your own design to the View list.

## Another way to change the current view

If you click the Contact toolbar's Organize button, Outlook gives you another way to change the view: click the Using Views hyperlink, and then select a view in the list box that Outlook supplies.

*continues*

## Contacts (continued)

### Looking Up a Contact in Address Cards View

Looking up a contact in Address Cards view is just like using a rotary file. You just spin the file, electronically, of course, until you find the card you want. To display your contacts in Address Cards view, choose the View menu's Current View command and the submenu's Address Cards command.

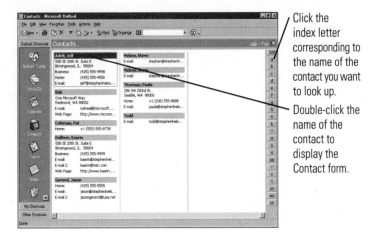

Click the index letter corresponding to the name of the contact you want to look up.

Double-click the name of the contact to display the Contact form.

### Look up a contact from any folder

You can quickly look up a contact from any folder by typing the contact's name in the Find A Contact text box on the Standard toolbar.

## Conversation Thread

A conversation thread is a **message** and all its **replies.** For example, if I send you an e-mail message that asks about a round of golf next Friday and you e-mail me a message saying that Friday doesn't work but Saturday sounds good, our two messages constitute a conversation thread.

Sometimes it's helpful to view the messages in a mail **folder** by conversation thread, so Outlook supplies a view called By Conversation Topic that lets you do that. To use this view, simply choose the View menu's Current View command and the submenu's By Conversation Topic command. To view the messages in a conversation thread, click the plus sign next to the conversation.

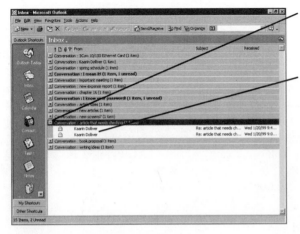

Click this button to expand or collapse the thread.

These messages constitute a thread.

**SEE ALSO** Newsreader; Views

## Copy

You can send someone a copy of a **message** that you're sending to someone else. All you need to do is enter the person's **e-mail name** in the Cc box. Or if you don't know the person's e-mail name, click Cc. When Outlook displays the Select Names dialog box (which shows the contents of your **Address Book** lists), use it to identify the person to whom you want to send the copy.

Enter the e-mail name of the person you want to receive the copy here.

**SEE ALSO** Blind Carbon Copy

## Custom Form

Outlook allows you to use custom forms to collect information from lots of different places. **Forms** sound funny at first, but they are actually very useful. You (or somebody else in your **organization**) might create an expense report form so that employees can describe and submit payment requests for reimbursable expenses. Or you might create a project status form so that the people working together can either report on or see how the project is progressing. You can create forms for all Outlook items (including **posts**) except Notes. You might even create a form that lets you share other, more entertaining information.

## Date Navigator

The Date Navigator is the small monthly calendar that appears in the upper right corner of the **Calendar** folder. You use the Date Navigator to pick the date or dates to display in the Calendar.

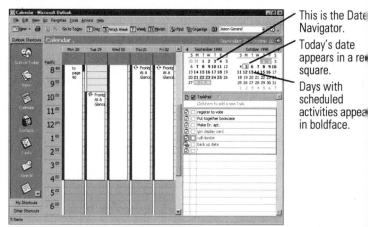

This is the Date Navigator.

Today's date appears in a red square.

Days with scheduled activities appear in boldface.

### Using the Date Navigator to Display Different Days' Schedules on the Calendar

Click a date to display that day's schedule in the Calendar. Drag the pointer over a series of dates to select them all, or select nonadjacent dates by holding down the Ctrl key and clicking each date.

### Moving from One Month to Another in Date Navigator

Click the left arrow to display the previous month; click the right arrow to display the next month. Click the month name in the Date Navigator's title bar, and a list of month names appears. Point above or below the list to scroll the list. Move the pointer over one of the month names and release the mouse button to display that month in the Date Navigator.

### Rescheduling an Appointment Using the Date Navigator

Simply drag a scheduled **appointment** from the Calendar to a date in the Date Navigator to reschedule an appointment for a different day.

## Deferred Delivery

You can tell Outlook to defer delivery of a message. In other words, you can say, "Okay, deliver this message, but not before some point in the future." To defer delivery of a message, display the message in a **Message form** and click the Options toolbar button. When Outlook displays the Message Options dialog box, select the Do Not Deliver Before check box and specify the deferral date.

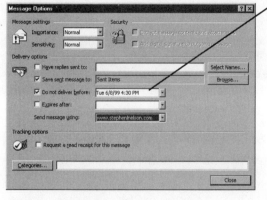

Enter the deferral date here.

This is a screen from the Internet Only version of Outlook; the Corporate or Workgroup version is slightly different.

## Defining Views SEE Views

## Delegate Access

When you're using Outlook as a Microsoft **Exchange Server** client, you can give other users on your network delegate access permissions. Delegate access permissions specify who can do what with your **Personal Folders**. For example, you can give other people on your network permission to view your **Calendar** and make or cancel appointments for you. Or you can give people permission to send and receive e-mail messages on your behalf. To add a delegate, choose the Tools menu's Options command, click the Delegates tab, and then click Add. Use the Add Users dialog box to select the name of the person to whom you want to give delegate access permissions. Then use the Delegate Permissions dialog box for that user to specify the permission level you want to give the delegate for each of your Personal Folders. Before you start fooling around with these settings, however, you might just want to check with your network administrator to see whether your company has policies regarding the delegate access feature and access permissions in general. It probably does.

## Delivery Receipt

The United States Postal Service, as you might know, offers a special service called registered mail. With registered mail, you get a delivery receipt, signed by the recipient, to prove that your letter or package truly reached its destination. Microsoft **Exchange Server** provides a similar service with its delivery receipts. You can ask the Exchange server to confirm that a **message** was delivered. To do this, click the Options toolbar button.

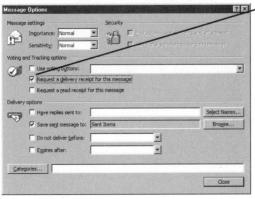

Select this check box to have Exchange tell you when it finishes delivering a message.

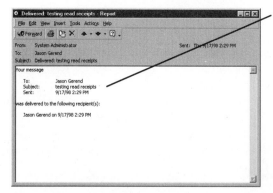

This is the type of message you'll receive that confirms the delivery of your message.

**SEE ALSO    Read Receipt**

# Digital ID

Digital IDs, or certificates, sign and sometimes seal a **message** so that its **recipient** can tell who really sent the message and be certain that no one tampered with the message en route.

### Using a Digital ID

To use a digital ID, you first sign up with a digital ID verification service. Microsoft Corporation recommends you use the VeriSign service. You can sign up for the VeriSign service by visiting the VeriSign web site at *www.verisign.com* and then following the site's onscreen instructions. (At this writing, you'll pay around $10 a year for the digital ID.)

After you sign up with the verification service and install the digital ID (following the verification service's instructions), you can send digitally signed messages to recipients. You can also encrypt messages to certain recipients.

To add a digital signature to a message, click the Options toolbar button and select the Add Digital Signature To Outgoing Message check box before you send the message. To seal a message with encryption, select the Encrypt Message Contents And Attachments check box. Click Close to close the Message Options dialog box, and then send the message in the usual way.

When you send a recipient a sealed or signed message, Outlook attaches a certificate to your message. The first time someone receives a certificate attachment, he or she needs to save the certificate. You save certificate attachments in the same way that you save other attachments. For example, you can right-click the attachment to display the shortcut menu and then choose the Save As command.

*continues*

## Digital ID *(continued)*

### Verifying a Digital Signature

Usually, when you open a digitally signed message, the certificate automatically appears so that you can immediately verify that the message hasn't been tampered with. If the certificate doesn't automatically open, choose the File menu's Properties command and click the Security tab.

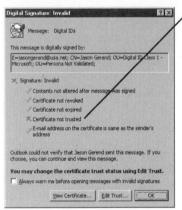

This message doesn't pass the test because its trust information isn't valid.

**SEE ALSO   Encryption; Security**

## Discussions  SEE  Post

## Distribution List

Using Outlook's **Address Book,** you can create a distribution list of people to whom you want to send a **message.** That sounds like no big deal, but distribution lists are actually pretty neat because they make it easy to send a message to a lot of people. Rather than separately listing the name of each **recipient** to whom you want to send a message, you just specify the distribution list.

### Creating a Distribution List

As long as you've already added the recipients to your **Contacts** folder or **Personal Address Book,** or you can find the recipients in the **Global Address List,** it's easy to create a long distribution list. To create the list, follow these steps:

**1** Click the down arrow next to the New Mail Message toolbar button, and then choose the drop-down menu's Distribution List command.

**2** Type a name for the list in the Distribution List Name text box.

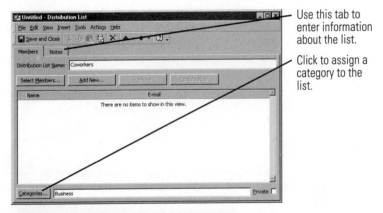

Use this tab to enter information about the list.

Click to assign a category to the list.

**3** Click Select Members to add contacts to your list.

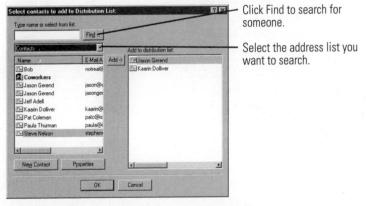

Click Find to search for someone.

Select the address list you want to search.

**4** Select a contact you want to add, and then click Add.

**5** When you're finished adding members, click OK, and then click the Save And Close toolbar button.

## Using a Distribution List

To send the same e-mail message to everyone named on a distribution list, just enter the distribution list name in the To box of the **Message form.**

## Drafts

By default, Outlook automatically saves messages you're writing to your Drafts folder every three minutes. And if you close a **message** without sending it, Outlook asks whether you want to save the message. If you indicate you do, Outlook keeps a copy of the partially completed message in your Drafts folder. To view the contents of the Drafts folder, click My Shortcuts on the **Outlook Bar** and then click the Drafts icon. To open a message that is stored in the Drafts folder, double-click it. To complete and send a message you've opened, make your changes and click the Send toolbar button.

## Electronic Mail SEE E-Mail

## E-Mail

E-mail is an abbreviation that stands for electronic mail. The term describes the **messages** that people send from one computer to another. In most cases, e-mail is transmitted instantaneously—or almost instantaneously. You send a message, and a few seconds or minutes later, someone receives it.

## E-Mail Alias

An e-mail alias is usually the same as an **e-mail name**. It's the name you use to send someone an e-mail message.

## E-Mail Etiquette

Good manners are never complicated, so you won't be surprised to learn that there's nothing particularly tricky about the etiquette of e-mail. Be courteous. Never say something you don't want repeated (or forwarded). Don't waste your recipient's time by sending useless messages or replies. In short, treat people as you yourself want to be treated, and respect their time.

## E-Mail Filters SEE Inbox Filters

## E-Mail Name

If you want to send me an e-mail **message**, you can't just type "Stephen L. Nelson" in the To box. My name might mean a lot to me, but to Outlook and the Internet, my name means hardly anything. What Outlook and the Internet use to uniquely identify me is my e-mail name. Steve, my e-mail name, does mean something. And if you sent an e-mail message to the Internet address *steve@stephenlnelson.com*, it would actually get to me.

## Encryption

When you encrypt something—like an e-mail **message**—you scramble the information so that it can't be read by anyone who doesn't know how to unscramble it. When the **recipient** gets your e-mail message, he or she decrypts, or unscrambles, it in order to read it. To encrypt messages, you need a **digital ID**. For someone on the Internet to read a message you've encrypted, you need to have first sent them a digital ID certificate.

## Eudora

Eudora is an e-mail client, just as Outlook is. This bit of information isn't all that relevant to this Pocket Guide—since it's about Outlook. But if you used to work with Eudora, you'll be interested to know that Outlook can probably grab both e-mail messages and e-mail names and addresses from Eudora so that you can use them in Outlook. Outlook does this, by the way, as you install it.

## Event

In Outlook an event is a notation in the **Calendar** that doesn't occupy a time slot. This sounds funny, but take the example of a birthday. You might want to note this event on your Calendar—so you remember to buy a gift, say—even though the event doesn't actually take time out of your work day. To put it another way, events are occasions that you want to remember but not necessarily schedule time for.

*continues*

## Event *(continued)*

### Creating an Event

To add an event to your Calendar, click the Calendar icon on the Outlook Bar.
Choose the Actions menu's New All Day Event command. Then use the Event
dialog box to describe the event and its timing.

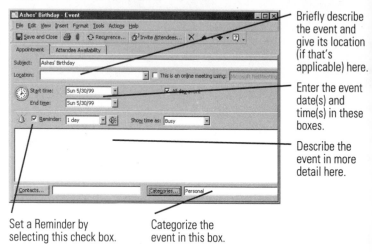

Briefly describe
the event and
give its location
(if that's
applicable) here.

Enter the event
date(s) and
time(s) in these
boxes.

Describe the
event in more
detail here.

Set a Reminder by
selecting this check box.

Categorize the
event in this box.

### Viewing Event Information

You can view event information in several ways. Outlook doesn't block out time on
your Calendar for events. Events appear on the Calendar as notices above the day
or days they are scheduled. You can also choose the View menu's Current View
command and then choose the submenu's Events command.

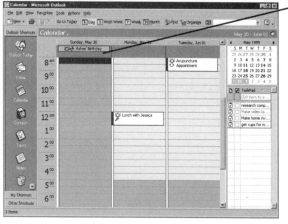

On the daily
Calendar, all-day
events show up
here.

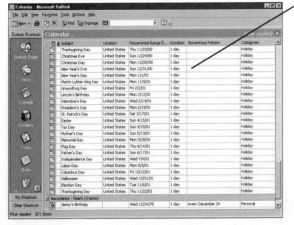

When you choose the Events view, all your scheduled events show up in a list.

## Exchange Server

Microsoft Exchange Server is software that runs on a network server. With Exchange and Outlook, you and the people you work with can pass messages around your network. Exchange also lets you coordinate people's schedules—figuring out, for example, when people next have time in their **Calendars** for a meeting.

**SEE ALSO    Plan A Meeting Wizard**

## Favorites Folder

The Favorites folder, a subfolder in the Windows folder, is a place where you can store files, shortcuts, or even other folders that you use frequently, so you know where to find them. In addition, Internet Explorer stores your favorite URLs in the Favorites folder. To view the contents of your Favorites folder using Outlook, click Other Shortcuts on the Outlook Bar and then click the Favorites icon.

*continues*

## Favorites Folder *(continued)*

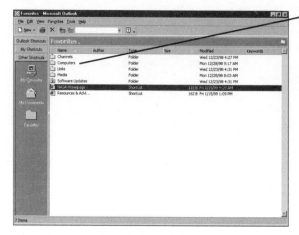

If your Favorites folder has subfolders, they show up on the Favorites list, too.

## Fax

If you have a fax/modem, you can use Outlook to send faxes to your contacts just as easily as you can send e-mail. If you are using the Internet Only version of Outlook, you use Symantec's WinFax Starter Edition to send faxes. If you're using the Corporate or Workgroup version of Outlook, you use the Microsoft Fax program. Each works slightly differently, but both are easy to use.

### Sending a Fax

To send a fax, click the down arrow next to the New Message toolbar button and then choose the pop-up menu's Fax Message command. Click the To button in the New Fax form, and choose a contact for whom you have a fax number recorded. Compose your message as you would an e-mail message, and then click the Send toolbar button when you're finished.

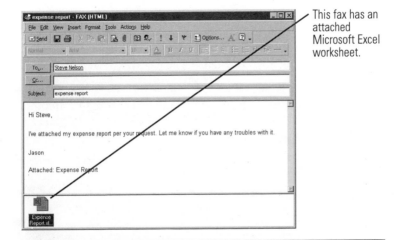

This fax has an attached Microsoft Excel worksheet.

## Setting Fax Options

To change how your faxes are sent and received, if you are using the Internet Only version of Outlook, choose the Tools menu's Options command and then click the Fax tab. If you are using the Corporate or Workgroup version of Outlook, choose the Tools menu's Services command, select Microsoft Fax, and then click Properties.

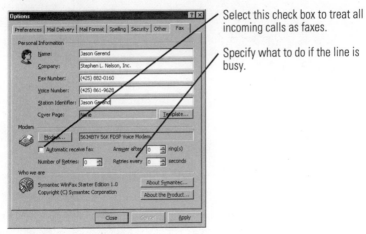

Select this check box to treat all incoming calls as faxes.

Specify what to do if the line is busy.

This is what the Fax options of the Internet Only version of Outlook look like.

# Field Chooser SEE Fields

# Fields

Outlook provides a variety of fields to describe details of particular items. You can add and remove fields from **views** of Outlook items. You can also create entirely new fields of your own.

In views that list items in a table format, such as the Messages view of the **Inbox,** fields are the **columns** of the table. In other types of views (such as the Address Cards view of the **Contacts** list), fields can appear as rows.

### Changing the Fields in a View

To change the fields displayed in a view, choose the View menu's Current View command and then choose the submenu's Customize Current View command. When Outlook displays the View Summary dialog box, click Fields. Outlook displays the Show Fields dialog box.

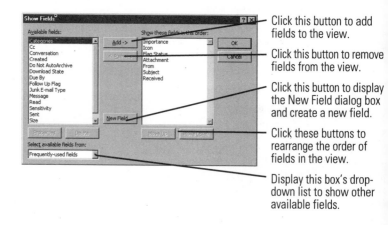

Click this button to add fields to the view.

Click this button to remove fields from the view.

Click this button to display the New Field dialog box and create a new field.

Click these buttons to rearrange the order of fields in the view.

Display this box's drop-down list to show other available fields.

**SEE ALSO**  Group By Box; Views

# File

A file is what you (and the computer **programs** you use) store on your computer's hard disk. As far as Outlook goes, you need to know two things about files: you can attach files to Outlook items (including the **messages** you send), and you can make it easier to share files on a network by copying the files into **Public Folders.**

**SEE ALSO**  Post

## Filters

Filters allow you to choose the items you want to display in the **information viewer**. Filters narrow down the list of items in a folder to just the ones that meet the criteria you set. To filter items, choose the View menu's Current View command and the submenu's Customize Current View command. When Outlook displays the View Summary dialog box, click Filter to display the Filter dialog box.

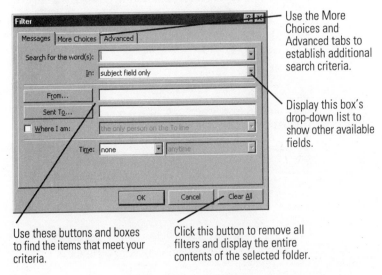

Use the More Choices and Advanced tabs to establish additional search criteria.

Display this box's drop-down list to show other available fields.

Use these buttons and boxes to find the items that meet your criteria.

Click this button to remove all filters and display the entire contents of the selected folder.

Outlook reminds you that you've filtered the information viewer by adding the words *Filter Applied* to the folder title bar.

**SEE ALSO**    **Inbox Filters; Task Filters; Views**

## Find

If you work in a large **organization** where everybody uses e-mail, if you maintain a long Contacts list, or if you're a manager who's constantly assigning tasks and attending meetings, the volume of items you need to track can be staggering. In such an environment, it's easy to lose or misplace items of importance. Fortunately, Outlook provides a powerful Find tool you can use in two ways to locate lost messages, tasks, contacts, and other items.

*continues*

## Find *(continued)*

### Finding Items

If you're pretty sure you know in which folder the item you're looking for is located, you can conduct a simple search for the item by displaying the item's folder and clicking the Find toolbar button to display the Find pane.

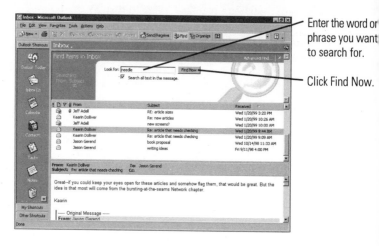

Enter the word or phrase you want to search for.

Click Find Now.

To conduct an advanced search for the item, choose the Tools menu's Advanced Find command and then use the Advanced Find dialog box.

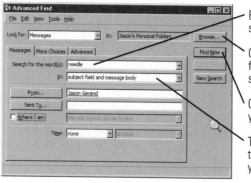

Enter the text you want to search for.

Click Browse to select the folders you want Outlook to search for the item.

Click Find Now to begin your search.

Tell Outlook what part of the item contains the text you entered.

### About the More Choices and Advanced tabs

You can specify additional search criteria on the More Choices and Advanced tabs. The More Choices tab lets you tell Outlook to look for items of a certain size or items that are assigned to a certain category. The Advanced tab allows you to add even more specific criteria.

### Finding Outlook Items Using the Start Menu

When you installed Outlook, Windows added a new command to the Find submenu on your Start menu: Using Microsoft Outlook. When you choose this command, Windows displays the Find dialog box so that you can search for Outlook items from anywhere in your computer without having to launch Outlook. You can also choose the Find submenu's On The Internet command to conduct an Internet search using a search service. Or you can choose the People command to find lost friends on the Internet using a directory service.

## Flame

A flame is an **e-mail message** that's mean and nasty. If you e-mail a message to me that says I'm a complete moron who is utterly incapable of constructing a sentence, for example, that's a flame. By the way, if I e-mail you back a message that says your mother wears army boots and your sister is ugly, we have what is known as a "flame war."

Flames, as you might guess, violate all the rules of e-mail good manners and etiquette. But because some people have the maturity of grade-schoolers, you see quite a few flames on the **Internet.** On a philosophical note, I suspect that the anonymity of e-mail and the Internet has something to do with this meanness. People are more apt to say mean and threatening things when they don't have to see the other person's face or worry about running into the other person at the grocery store or a staff meeting.

## Folder

Outlook uses folders to organize Outlook items. The Inbox and Outbox folders store message items you've received or plan to send. The Contacts folder stores contact items. The Tasks folder stores task items, and so on.

By the way, it's easy to create new folders. Select the folder or mailbox in which you want to place a new folder. Then choose the File menu's New command and the submenu's Folder command.

*continues*

## Folder *(continued)*

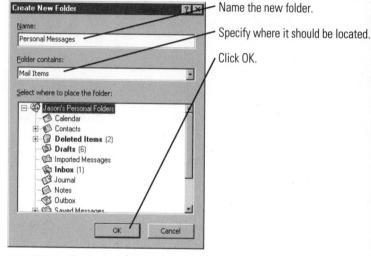

Name the new folder.

Specify where it should be located.

Click OK.

**SEE ALSO  Folder Banner; Folder List; Outlook Folders; Subfolder**

## Folder Banner

The Folder Banner is the bar below the toolbars in the Outlook window. On the left side of the Folder Banner, Outlook displays the name of the selected folder. You can click the folder name to display a list of all the **Outlook folders.** The Folder Banner also displays the selected folder's icon and additional information such as today's date in the **Calendar** or the alphabetical range of contacts displayed in the **Contacts** folder.

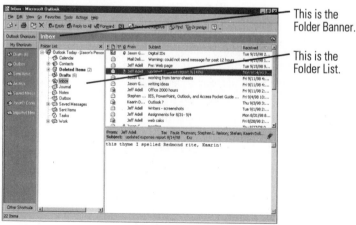

This is the Folder Banner.

This is the Folder List.

# Folder List

The term *Folder List* refers to the folder tree, or hierarchy, that Outlook displays in the left portion of the Outlook window. If you've worked with Outlook for more than a day or two, you already know that Outlook uses these **folders** to organize various **items**.

In addition, you can use Outlook just like you'd use Windows Explorer or My Computer—to display the folder hierarchy of your entire computer and network. If the Folder List doesn't appear in the Outlook program window and you want to see it, click the folder name on the **Folder Banner**.

**SEE ALSO   Outlook Folders**

# Folder View

A Folder view is a certain way to look at the information in a specific **folder**. For example, you can organize the **messages** in the **Inbox** folder by specifying which **columns** (or **fields**) appear, how messages are grouped or sorted, and whether any e-mail **filters** are used. Outlook offers a variety of predefined Folder **views**.

### Creating a Folder View

To create a Folder view, choose the View menu's Current View command and the submenu's Define Views command. When Outlook displays the Define Views dialog box, click New. Outlook displays the Create A New View dialog box.

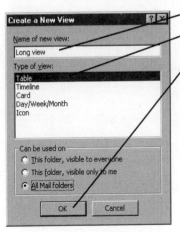

Name your new view.

Specify the type of view and where it can be used.

When you click OK, Outlook displays the View Summary dialog box.

*continues*

## Folder View *(continued)*

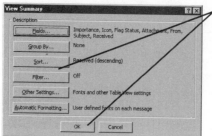

Click these buttons to specify the columns of message information (fields), grouping, sorting, filtering, and formatting you want. Then click OK.

### Using a Folder View

To see and select a predefined view, choose the View menu's Current View command and then choose one of the submenu's commands.

**SEE ALSO    Fields; Grouping Items; Sorting**

## Font

If you've worked with a word processor—say, Microsoft **Word**—you probably know that a font is simply a typeface that looks a certain way. What you may not know is that Outlook easily passes back and forth **HTML** and Rich Text Files (RTF) files, which let you include all sorts of fonts in messages.

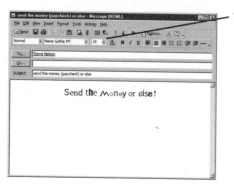

This is the Formatting toolbar.

It's easy to format a **message.** With the **Message form** displayed, select the text and then click the Formatting toolbar's buttons and open the drop-down list boxes to make your changes. You can use the Font box to change the current text selection's font, for example. And you can use the Font Size box to specify the font point size. You can also use the Format menu's Font command to make changes to a font. When you choose this command, Outlook displays the Font dialog box. You can use it to make your formatting changes.

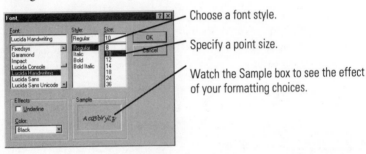

Choose a font style.

Specify a point size.

Watch the Sample box to see the effect of your formatting choices.

## Form

In Outlook, you use forms to collect and view information. For example, when you create a **message,** you use a form called the **Message form.** In this form you name the **recipient,** enter the message **subject,** and type in the **message body.** Outlook comes with predefined forms for writing and reading **e-mail** messages, of course. But you can create specialized forms for collecting and viewing other types of information, too: employee expense reports, project schedule updates, and so on.

**SEE ALSO**   **Custom Form**

## Form Design

You can create your own customized **forms** by choosing the Tools menu's Forms command and the submenu's Design A Form command. You probably don't need to design a form, however, because Outlook provides almost all the forms most users could ever need.

**SEE ALSO   Custom Form**

## Forward

You can send a copy of a **message** you receive to someone else. To do this, select or display the message and then click the Forward toolbar button. Outlook opens a **form** that you use to create your response.

## Free Time SEE Busy Time

## Global Address List

If you work on a network that includes an **Exchange server,** the Global Address List lists all the people in your **organization** to whom you can send e-mail. The Global Address List can be viewed by clicking the Address Book toolbar button and then selecting Global Address List from the Show Names From The drop-down list box.

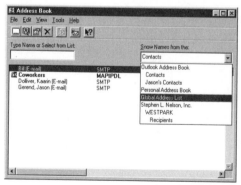

If your organization is huge, with hundreds or thousands of users, the Global Address List isn't a useful way to find the e-mail names of people with whom you regularly correspond. Instead, add your regular correspondents' e-mail names to your **Contacts** folder.

## Group By Box

If you've chosen to display the Advanced toolbar—you can do this by choosing the View menu's Toolbars command and then choosing Advanced—you can group and ungroup **messages** and **tasks** in the Group By box. To use the Group By box, click the Group By Box toolbar button. Outlook opens a space—the Group By box—between the **Folder Banner** and the column headings of the **information viewer.** You can drag column headings, which are actually buttons, in and out of the Group By box to group items by those headings. Outlook groups items based on the order in which the headings appear in the box. If you don't like the order, simply rearrange the headings. And when you want to ungroup items, just drag the headings back into the information viewer.

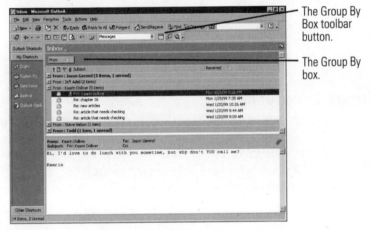

The Group By Box toolbar button.

The Group By box.

**SEE ALSO   Grouping Items; Views**

## Grouping Items

You can tell Outlook to group **items** with similar characteristics. For example, you can tell Outlook to group **messages** with the same **sender,** the same **subject,** and so on. To do this, choose the View menu's Current View command and the submenu's Customize Current View command. When Outlook displays the View Summary dialog box, click Group By. Outlook displays the Group By dialog box, which you can use to specify how you want to group items such as messages.

*continues*

### Grouping Items *(continued)*

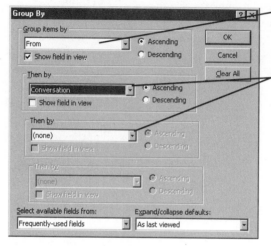

Specify how you want items grouped by using the Group Items By drop-down list box.

You can group items within a group by using the Then By list boxes.

**SEE ALSO    Group By Box**

## Group Scheduling

You can use Outlook to schedule meetings for groups of people as long as everybody uses an **iCalendar**-compatible program or is on the same **Exchange Server** network and uses either Outlook or Microsoft **Schedule+** to keep their appointment calendars. To perform such group scheduling, use the **Plan A Meeting Wizard.**

## Help

Outlook's online help feature gives you information with just a mouse click or a keystroke. You can access the conventional help system by choosing the Help menu's Microsoft Outlook Help command. You also have another source of help, the **Office Assistant,** Microsoft Office's animated help feature. When you click the Office Assistant toolbar button or choose the Help menu's Microsoft Outlook Help command, Outlook starts the Office Assistant.

## History

Outlook maintains a history of the documents you've opened. You can view this history from either the Open or Save As dialog boxes by clicking the History shortcut.

## HTML

The acronym HTML stands for hypertext markup language. HTML is what you use to create **World Wide Web** documents or to send richly formatted e-mail messages.

**SEE ALSO    Font; HTML Stationery**

## HTML Mail

HTML Mail has become the standard format for formatted e-mail messages. Outlook 2000 sends and receives industry-standard e-mail messages formatted in **HTML**. Although HTML-formatted e-mail is the industry standard, some people (such as many college students) still do not use e-mail programs capable of viewing HTML files. When in doubt, it's best to send a message formatted in Plain Text.

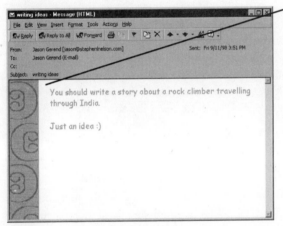

This e-mail includes HTML formatting.

**SEE ALSO    Message Format; Stationery**

## Hyperlink

You can insert a link to a **World Wide Web** page or FTP site—a hyperlink—in your messages. You just need to know the **URL**, or hyperlink address, of the **web page** or FTP site to which you want to link. To insert a hyperlink in a message, type the hyperlink address in the message area of the **Message form**. The hyperlink becomes active as soon as you finish typing it.

*continues*

## Hyperlink *(continued)*

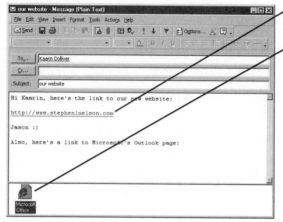

This is a hyperlink to a web page.

This is a shortcut to a web page.

If you've been using your **web browser** to collect favorite web pages in your Favorites folder, you can take advantage of the URL addresses stored in your Favorites folder to insert a shortcut to a web page in your messages. To do this, click the Other Shortcuts group on the Outlook Bar and then click the Favorites shortcut icon. Right-click the shortcut you want to insert, and choose the shortcut menu's Copy command. Then, in a message window, click the Paste toolbar button to insert the shortcut.

**SEE ALSO    Internet**

## iCalendar

The iCalendar is an industry-standard file format that allows users of different calendar programs to share their calendar information and schedule appointments. Outlook is one of the first programs to support the use of this important new standard. Using iCalendar, people and companies can post their schedules on their web sites, allowing others to view their schedules and plan meeting times that work for all parties involved.

To use iCalendar to publish your calendar information and to view others' information, you need to have a web site where you can post your iCalendar file.

To send an appointment as an iCalendar file, select the appointment in your **Calendar** and then choose the Actions menu's Forward As iCalendar command to open a new mail message with the iCalendar file attached.

To receive an iCalendar file, simply double-click the iCalendar file, review the appointment information, and then click the Save And Close toolbar button to save the information to your own Calendar.

**SEE ALSO**   Calendar; Startup Wizard

## MAP

IMAP stands for Internet Message Access Protocol and was designed by my alma mater, the University of Washington, to allow users to access their e-mail messages from multiple locations. IMAP does this by storing all messages on your mail server, allowing you to view them from any location. POP, or Post Office Protocol, differs from IMAP by forcing you to download messages to your computer. Once downloaded, they are unavailable for viewing from another computer unless you specified to leave a copy on the **server**.

IMAP is supported by Outlook, but only if you install the **Internet Only** version.

**SEE ALSO**   Startup Wizard

## mportance

Some of the **messages** you send are very important either to you or the **recipient.** And some of the messages aren't important at all. To deal with differences in urgency and importance, you can assign a priority, or level of importance, to the messages you write. Unless you tell it otherwise, Outlook assumes your message is of normal importance. To assign high importance to a message, click the Importance: High toolbar button. To assign low importance, click the (you guessed it) Importance: Low toolbar button. You can also assign importance and indicate a message's sensitivity by clicking the Options toolbar button when the Message form is displayed.

*continues*

## Importance *(continued)*

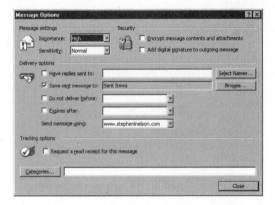

Messages' importance level and sensitivity show up in the recipient's **information viewer,** which helps the recipient identify urgent and important messages. By the way, Microsoft **Exchange Server** can be set up to deliver high-priority messages faster.

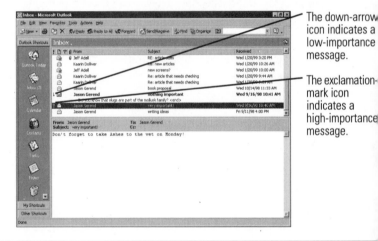

The down-arrow icon indicates a low-importance message.

The exclamation-mark icon indicates a high-importance message.

## Import and Export

Outlook provides the Import And Export Wizard to help you import items and files from other applications into Outlook and export items and files from Outlook to other applications. For example, if you have a file in another personal information manager that contains names and addresses of business contacts, you can use the Import And Export Wizard to move that information into Outlook.

## Importing Data Not Previously Imported

To import a file from another program, follow these steps:

**1** Choose the File menu's Import And Export command. Outlook displays the Import And Export Wizard dialog box.

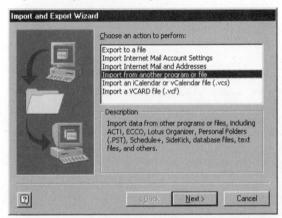

**2** Select Import From Another Program Or File in the Choose An Action To Perform list box. Then click Next. Outlook displays the Import A File dialog box.

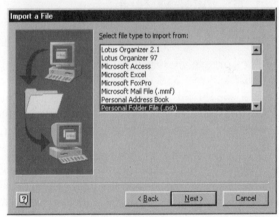

**3** Select the type of data file you want to import in the Select File Type To Import From list box, and then click Next.

**4** If Outlook does not find the correct file, click Browse to locate the file you want to import.

**5** Specify how Outlook should deal with duplicate items, and then click Next.

**6** In the final Import A File dialog box, check to make sure that Outlook will import the items you want. Click Finish.

**SEE ALSO** Calendar; Contacts

## Inbox

The Inbox is the **Outlook folder** that receives and holds incoming **messages.** To view your Inbox, click the Inbox icon on the **Outlook Bar** or the Inbox folder icon in the **Folder List.**

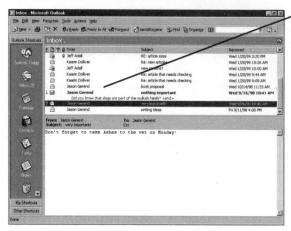

The Inbox folder lists all the messages people have sent to you.

## Inbox Assistant SEE **Rules Wizard**

## Inbox Filters

You can filter, or hide, **messages** that appear in the **information viewer** so that only messages with specific characteristics appear. For example, you can filter the information viewer so that only messages from particular **senders** get listed. Or you can filter messages so that only those marked as important or those with **attachments** get listed.

To filter messages, select the **folder** with the messages you want to filter, choose the View menu's Current View command, and then choose the submenu's Customize Current View command. When Outlook displays the View Summary dialog box, click Filter. Outlook displays the Filter dialog box, which you use to describe how you want to filter messages.

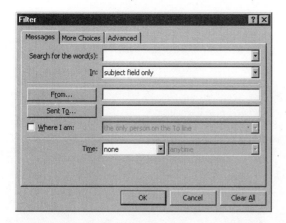

## Filtering Messages by Sender

To filter messages by sender, first use the From box to specify the name of the sender whose messages you want to see. If you don't know the sender's **e-mail name,** click From to display the **Address Book** and use it to identify the sender. You can, by the way, specify more than one sender—all you need to do is separate their e-mail names with semicolons.

## Filtering Messages by Recipient

You can filter messages by **recipient,** too, although you wouldn't do this with the messages in your Inbox folder. (In your **Inbox,** you are the recipient.) To filter messages by recipient, use the Sent To box to specify the name of the recipient whose messages you want to see. If you don't know the recipient's e-mail name, click Sent To to display the Address Book and use it to identify the recipient. If you specify more than one recipient, separate their e-mail names with semicolons.

Select the Where I Am check box, and select The Only Person On The To Line from the drop-down list box to see only those messages that name you specifically as the recipient (rather than name a **distribution list** on which your name appears). Or select On The Cc Line With Other People to see only those messages that are actually copies of messages sent to another recipient.

*continues*

## Inbox Filters *(continued)*

### Filtering Messages by Subject and Text

You can filter messages on the basis of their **subjects** or the text in the **message body.** To filter messages in these ways, enter a snippet of text in the Search For The Word(s) box. Then, using the In box, tell Outlook to search for the word(s) in the subject field only or in the subject field and message body.

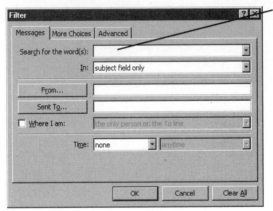

To see only messages that have something to do with golf, type the word *golf* in the Search For The Word(s) box.

### Filtering Messages by Category

You can filter messages based on the **categories** you assigned them. Click the More Choices tab of the Filter dialog box. Click Categories, and then select the message categories you want in the Available Categories list. Click OK twice to filter the information viewer by category.

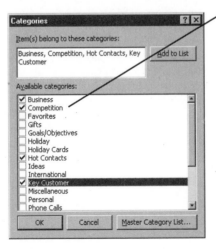

Choose one or more categories to narrow down a list of messages.

## About the Clear All button and the Advanced tab

The Filter dialog box provides numerous other choices—let me quickly describe two of them. You can click Clear All to remove all of the filters in the Filter dialog box. And you can click the Advanced tab to display boxes and buttons for filtering messages even more precisely.

> **SEE ALSO**   Filters; Task Filters; Views

## Information Service

The Corporate or Workgroup version of Outlook uses information services to send and receive **e-mail**, pass information between the **Outlook client** and an **Exchange server**, and get address information. If you want to send e-mail using an account with an **Internet service provider**, for example, you use an information service. If you want to connect to an Exchange server that's part of your local area network—perhaps so you can get a coworker's e-mail address from the **Global Address List**—you use an information service.

Let me tell you three more things about information services. First, you don't install information services using Outlook or the Outlook setup program. You install an information service from a network server (like an Exchange server) or by using a separate disk that supplies an e-mail account setup program. Second, you can't use an information service until it's been added to your **profile.** Third, you look at, make minor changes to your computer's information services, and add services to your profile by using the Tools menu's Services command. (To do this, choose the Tools menu's Services command, click Add, and then when Outlook displays its list of installed services, double-click the name of the service you want to add.)

> **SEE ALSO**   Internet Only; Startup Wizard

## Information Viewer

The term *information viewer* refers to the right portion of the Outlook program window. The information viewer shows the **items** stored in the selected **folder.**

*continues*

## Information Viewer *(continued)*

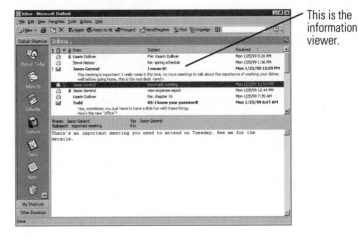

This is the information viewer.

**SEE ALSO    Columns; Fields; Preview Pane**

## Internet

Once you understand that a **network** is just a bunch of computers that are connected so that information, including e-mail **messages,** can be shared, it's easy to understand what the Internet is: the Internet is a network of networks. If you have an Internet connection (through an **Internet service provider,** for example) or if your **organization's** network is connected to the Internet, you can use Outlook to easily send e-mail to anybody else connected to the Internet. (You do need to know the recipient's **e-mail name,** however.)

**SEE ALSO    Hyperlink; URL; World Wide Web**

## Internet Explorer

Outlook comes with a copy of Microsoft's web browser, Internet Explorer. Using Internet Explorer, you can view web pages and even access other Internet resources.

**SEE ALSO    Outlook Express**

## Internet Only

The Internet Only version of Outlook is the version of Outlook optimized for sending and receiving Internet e-mail. When you install the Internet Only version of Outlook, you can use features that users of the Corporate or Workgroup version cannot use, such as **IMAP** folders. You also use Symantec WinFax Starter Edition to **fax**. However, as an Internet Only version user you cannot use workgroup features such as **Exchange servers**, **Remote Mail**, and **Public Folders**.

**SEE ALSO**   **Startup Wizard**

## Internet Service Provider

An Internet service provider, or ISP, is a company that lets you connect to its Internet host, usually for a fee.

One point that's a little bit confusing but important to understand is that you pay an Internet service provider merely to *access* the Internet. You're not paying anything to *use* the Internet. To use the information superhighway analogy, Internet service providers set up tollbooths that you must go through before you can get on the highway. But you actually use the highway for free.

Let me give you a few tips on picking an Internet service provider. First, check prices. You can pay anywhere from $10 to around $50 a month for an Internet service provider's service. (To keep your costs down, you'll want to choose a local provider to save on long-distance telephone charges.) Second, you should verify that you'll be able to connect when you want. (You can test this just by trying to connect a few times before you actually sign up.) Finally, if you're interested in creating your own web site, you should ask if they give you a free web site, how much hard disk space they provide on their server, and if they have Microsoft FrontPage **Server Extensions**.

**SEE ALSO**   **Newsreader**

## Intranet

The **Internet,** it turns out, uses lots of special rules and conventions, called protocols, for sharing information and equipment. Because the Internet's protocols allow you to do some pretty neat things—including create web pages—some **organizations** use these protocols on their own internal networks. Outsiders can't use these internal networks because these networks aren't part of the Internet. But because these internal networks work like the Internet, people call them intranets.

**SEE ALSO   Hyperlink; URL; World Wide Web**

## Items

In Outlook, each **appointment, contact, Journal** entry, meeting, **message, Note,** or **task** is called an **item.** You can act upon items in a variety of ways: for example, you can **copy,** delete, **filter, forward, group,** move, print, send, and **sort** items.

## Item-Specific Menu SEE Actions

## Journal

The Journal is an **Outlook folder** that tracks your daily activities and displays them on a timeline. If the activity you want to track is an Outlook **item,** such as a phone call to a contact, you can tell the Journal to record it automatically. You can even have the Journal automatically record Microsoft **Word** documents, Microsoft Excel spreadsheets, and Microsoft Access databases that you create.

If you want to track an activity that has nothing whatever to do with Outlook, you can still use the Journal by adding entries to the Journal manually.

In Outlook 2000, to get to the Journal, click the My Shortcuts group on the Outlook Bar and click the Journal icon.

Journal entries appear as icons on the timeline. After you've recorded several activities, your Journal timeline appears something like the one shown on the next page.

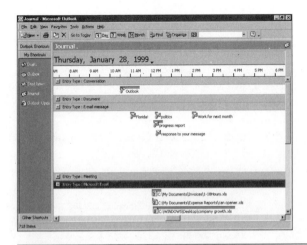

## Using the Journal to Automatically Track Interactions with Contacts

Using the Journal, you can keep track of **e-mail** messages and faxes you send to and receive from selected **contacts**. You can also record meeting and task requests to and responses from your contacts.

To automatically record interactions with existing contacts, follow these steps:

**1** Choose the Tools menu's Options command. Outlook displays the Options dialog box.

**2** Click the Preferences tab, and then click Journal Options.

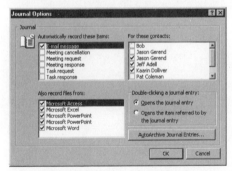

**3** In the Automatically Record These Items box, check the items you want to automatically record in the Journal.

**4** In the For These Contacts box, check the names of the contacts you want to record your interactions with.

**5** Click OK. Outlook will make a Journal entry any time you interact in the indicated manner with any of the contacts you selected.

*continues*

73

## Journal *(continued)*

### Using the Journal to Record Documents You Create

To record any new files you create in other Microsoft Office programs, choose the Tools menu's Options command, click Journal Options, and then check the names of the programs you want to track in the Also Record Files From box.

### Using the Journal to Record Phone Calls to Contacts

Whenever you call a contact using Outlook's **AutoDial** feature, you can make a record of the phone call. This could come in handy for billing a customer for time spent on the phone, for instance, or simply to jog your memory later.

To record a phone call to a contact, select the contact and choose the Actions menu's Call Contact command. Then select the phone number you want to dial for the contact. Outlook displays the New Call dialog box.

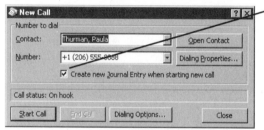 Select this check box to record a Journal entry for a phone call.

Click Start Call, and Outlook displays the Call Status dialog box. Click Talk, pick up your phone, and Outlook displays the Phone Call form.

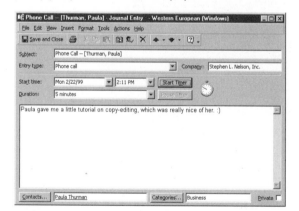

Click Start Timer to keep track of the length of the call. When the call is complete, click Pause Timer and click End Call. You can type notes about the call in the text area of the form either while the call is in progress or after you hang up. When you've finished writing notes, click the Save And Close toolbar button.

## Manually Recording Outlook Items in the Journal

To manually record any Outlook item in the Journal, just drag the item to the Journal icon. Outlook displays the Journal Entry form for the item.

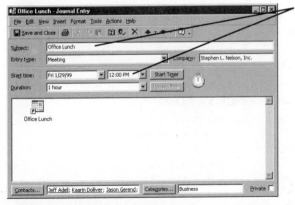

Fill in the text boxes to describe the meeting.

## Manually Recording Miscellaneous Activities in the Journal

You can make a record of just about anything you want in the Journal. Display the Journal, and click the New Journal Entry toolbar button. Outlook displays the Untitled—Journal Entry form. Describe the entry type, and then fill out the rest of the boxes to describe the activity or event. Then click the Save And Close toolbar button to record it in the Journal.

# Junk E-Mail

If you send mail over the **Internet,** sooner or later you're bound to get the electronic equivalent of junk mail. (You'll begin to get junk e-mail almost immediately, by the way, if you **post** messages to newsgroups.) To help you deal with junk e-mail, Outlook includes a special command, Add To Junk Senders List. This command tells Outlook to automatically delete any e-mail you get from a particular e-mail address or alias. To use this command, display the **Inbox,** right-click a junk e-mail message, and choose the shortcut menu's Junk E-Mail command. Then choose the submenu's Add To Junk Senders List command. To add senders to your Adult Content Senders list, choose the submenu's Add To Adult Content Senders List command.

*continues*

## Junk E-Mail *(continued)*

Outlook's Organize pane lets you create rules that tell Outlook what to do with the mail you receive from people on your Junk Senders and Adult Content Senders lists. You can tell Outlook to display junk e-mail messages in a different color or to automatically move these messages to another folder. To create such rules, display your Inbox and click the Organize toolbar button. Then click the Junk E-Mail tab.

### Viewing Junk E-Mail Lists

To view your Junk Senders or Adult Content Senders lists, click the Junk E-Mail tab of the Organize pane. Then click the hyperlink to view more Junk E-Mail options. Click the Edit Junk Senders or Edit Adult Content Senders hyperlink to edit or remove senders on these lists.

## Kilobit

A kilobit is 1,024 bits, which is relevant because modem speeds are usually measured in kilobits. Don't confuse the terms *kilobit* and *kilobyte*. It takes eight kilobits to make one kilobyte.

## Kilobyte

I know you didn't buy this book to learn about the guts of your computer. But since I've used the term *kilobyte* in a couple of places, I thought I should at least define it. A byte is an eight-digit string of 1s and 0s that your computer uses to represent a character. (These 1s and 0s are called bits.) This, for example, is a byte:

01010100

A kilobyte is roughly 1,000 of these bytes. (Or to be precise, a kilobyte is exactly 1,024 of these bytes.)

## Laptop

A laptop is a portable computer designed to be small enough to fit on your lap. If you have a laptop, there are a few features in Outlook that might help you. If you need to read e-mail from more than one computer, you might be interested in using **IMAP** folders for your e-mail. You might also be interested in the Personal Folders Synchronization Wizard. And if you work on a network with an **Exchange server**, you might be interested in using **Remote Mail** and **Offline Folders.**

## Mailbox

If you're using Outlook as part of a network, a mailbox is the location on the server where your **messages** get delivered. Your network administrator sets up a mailbox for you and then you add the mailbox to your profile to view the messages in your mailbox.

## Mail Folders

Mail folders include all the folders dealing with Outlook's **e-mail** functions—Inbox, Outbox, Sent Items, and Deleted Items. Messages you've received are stored in the **Inbox** folder. Messages you've sent are stored in the Sent Items folder. Messages you've sent that haven't yet been delivered to the **server** are stored in the Outbox folder. You may also have other Mail folders that you created to store **junk e-mail** or a group of messages you want to set aside and save in their own folder. You can open a Mail folder by clicking its icon on the **Outlook Bar** or in the **Folder List.**

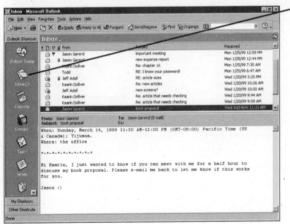

To see the messages in a folder, click its icon.

# Message

Messages are the e-mails and faxes you send with Outlook. The great thing about Outlook is the power it gives you to work with your messages.

### Writing a Message

To write a message, if you're already in the Inbox, click the New Mail Message toolbar button. Otherwise, click the down-arrow next to the New Item toolbar button (the button changes depending upon which Outlook folder you're in), and choose the Mail Message command. Outlook displays the **Message form.** (If you use the default Outlook e-mail text editor, your Message form looks much like the one shown below.) To continue writing your message, follow these steps:

**1** Enter the e-mail name of the recipient.

**2** If you want someone else to get a **copy** of the message, enter his or her e-mail name.

**3** Briefly describe your message.

**4** Type your message text.

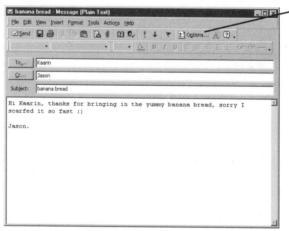

Click the Options toolbar button to set general message options (such as Importance) and other delivery and tracking options.

### Attaching a File to a Message

Many messages include only text typed in the Message form. But you can also **attach** a **file** to a message. In this way, you can include items in your e-mail such as word-processed documents, spreadsheets, and anything else you can store as a file on your hard disk. To attach a file, click the Insert File toolbar button. When Outlook displays the Insert File dialog box, name the file and identify its disk location.

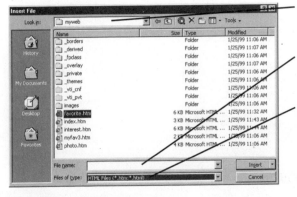

Identify the file's disk location in the Look In box.

Enter the file's name in the File Name box.

Select an entry in the Files Of Type list box that specifies the types of files you want to see listed in the Insert File dialog box.

## You have a choice

You get a choice as to the way Outlook attaches a file to your message. Click the down arrow to the right of the Insert toolbar button. If your file contains only unformatted text and you just want to insert the text in your message, choose Insert As Text from the drop-down menu. (It tells Outlook to insert the file as a text file in your message—something you would do only with text files.) If your file contains more than unformatted text, choose either Insert As Attachment or Insert As Shortcut. Choosing Insert As Attachment tells Outlook to insert an actual copy of the file in the message. The Insert As Shortcut option is available only for messages created using Microsoft Outlook Rich Text mail format. The Insert As Shortcut option inserts a shortcut icon in your message that points to a file on a computer. When Outlook later sends the message, it uses this shortcut to find the file with the actual message. (The recipient must have access to the location where the file is stored.)

### Attaching Other Items to a Message

You can attach any existing Outlook item to a message. In other words, you can insert other messages, **Calendar** files, **Contacts** list items, **Notes,** and so forth. To do this, choose the Insert menu's Item command. When Outlook displays the Insert Item dialog box, identify the item you want to send and tell Outlook how you want it inserted.

*continues*

## Message *(continued)*

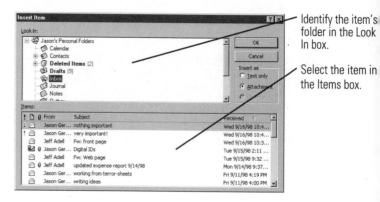

Identify the item's folder in the Look In box.

Select the item in the Items box.

---

### Sending a Message Over a Local Area Network

After you write a message, send it by clicking the Send toolbar button. If your computer connects to a network that includes an **Exchange server,** Outlook sends your message to the recipient you named. In a few minutes—maybe sooner—they receive the message.

---

### Sending a Message Over the Internet

If your computer connects to the **Internet** and that's how you send and receive messages, clicking the Send toolbar button tells Outlook to place the message in your Outbox folder. To move the message out of your Outbox and to the mail server you use to send and receive e-mail, click the Send And Receive toolbar button. Or, alternatively, if you have more than one **Internet service provider** and you want to select one for sending the message, choose the Tools menu's Send And Receive command. When Outlook displays the Send And Receive submenu, choose the Internet service provider you want to use from the submenu. Outlook makes the connection to the Internet service provider and then sends and receives any Internet e-mail messages.

---

### Reading Your Messages

To read the messages that other people have sent you, display the **Inbox** folder by clicking its icon on the **Outlook Bar.** Outlook lists any messages you've received. Unread messages are displayed in boldface. To view a message, double-click it. When you do this, Outlook displays the message in its own window.

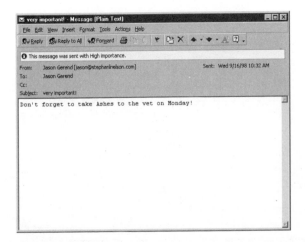

When you finish reading a message, just close the window. This tells Outlook to leave the message in your Inbox folder and not do anything else with it. Alternatively, you can click the Delete toolbar button. This tells Outlook to move the message to the Deleted Items folder. (Presumably, you move messages to the Deleted Items folder as a last stop before you remove them forever by choosing the Tools menu's Empty "Deleted Items" Folder command.)

### Replying to a Message

It's easy to reply to messages that others have sent you. To do this, click either the Reply or the Reply To All toolbar buttons. The Reply toolbar button tells Outlook you want to send a message only to the person who originally sent the message to you. The Reply To All toolbar button tells Outlook you want to send a message to the original sender and to everyone else who received a copy of the message. After you click either the Reply or Reply To All toolbar buttons, Outlook opens a new Message form that holds a copy of the original message and names the recipients to whom you want to send the message. Type your reply, and click the Send toolbar button.

*continues*

## Message *(continued)*

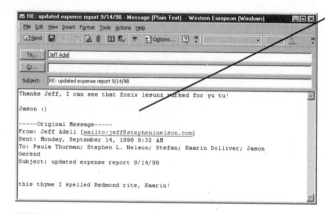

Whatever you type in your reply message gets inserted here.

### Forwarding a Message

It's easy to forward a message you received from someone else. First either select the message in the Outlook window by clicking it or display the message in a separate window. Next click the Forward toolbar button. Outlook opens a Message form that holds a copy of the original message.

Specify to whom you want to forward the message by entering the e-mail name. (Click To to open your **Address Book**.)

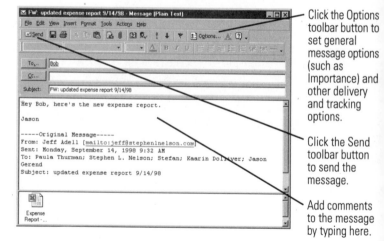

Click the Options toolbar button to set general message options (such as Importance) and other delivery and tracking options.

Click the Send toolbar button to send the message.

Add comments to the message by typing here.

## Printing a Message

You can print the messages you write and receive. To do this, just select the message and click the Print toolbar button.

If you want more control over how your message is printed, choose the File menu's Print command. When Outlook displays the Print dialog box, choose a printer, tell Outlook how many copies to print, describe what Outlook should do about any attachments, and so forth.

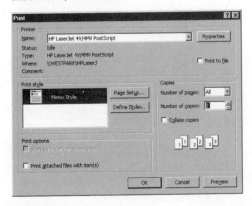

# Message Body

The message body is the actual message. In other words, it's the text element of the message, not the **e-mail name** of the **sender** or the **recipient** or the message **subject**.

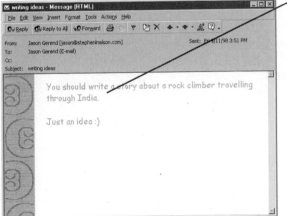

This block of text is the message body.

## Message Expiration

You can tell Outlook that a message should expire if a recipient hasn't read it by a certain date or time. In other words, you can say, "Okay, deliver this message—but if the recipient doesn't read it by some point in the future, make the message unavailable for reading." To set an expiration date for a message, display the message in a Message form and click the Options toolbar button. When Outlook displays the Message Options dialog box, select the Expires After check box and specify a date.

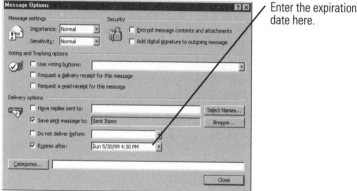

Enter the expiration date here.

## Message Flag

When you flag a message, you mark it with a flag icon, either to remind yourself to take further action or to ask someone else to act. Message flags appear in two places: as a message bar added to the **Message form** itself and in the Flag Status **column** of the Message view of the Inbox **information viewer.**

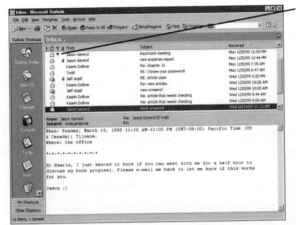

The message flag appears here.

Outlook has several predefined message flags: Call, Follow Up, Forward, Read, Reply, Reply To All, or Review. Or you can invent a message flag of your own. You can also set a due date by which you want the suggested action taken.

---

### Flagging a Message

To flag a message, open an existing message or click the New Mail Message toolbar button. Then click the Flag For Follow Up toolbar button. Outlook displays the Flag For Follow Up dialog box.

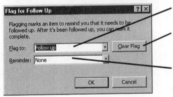

Select a flag from this box.

Click Clear Flag to remove a flag previously set.

To set a Reminder date, enter it here.

## Message Form

The Message form is the window Outlook displays that you can use to write **e-mail messages.** Why it's called a **form** instead of a window is sometimes confusing. But all you need to understand is that Outlook calls the windows you use to enter information—such as an e-mail message—forms. In the case of an e-mail message, "form" doesn't fit the bill very well. For the **custom forms** that Outlook lets you create, however, "form" works quite nicely. You can create forms, for example, for reporting employee business expenses. (In this case, employees would fill out business expense forms and e-mail them to the accountant.)

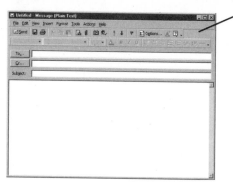

This is the Message form. You can also call it the Message Form window.

## Message Format

Outlook gives you three different choices for the editor you use to create new e-mail messages: **HTML,** Microsoft Outlook Rich Text, and Plain Text. The editor you choose determines the message formatting options you have available. To select a message editor, choose the Tools menu's Options command and click the Mail Format tab. Then select an editor in the Message Format drop-down list box.

But which editor should you choose? Well, it depends on the e-mail setups of the people with whom you most regularly communicate. For example, if you know that most of your message recipients have newer e-mail programs that can read HTML-formatted mail, you might want to choose HTML so that you can make use of Outlook's **stationery.** HTML format has one major drawback, however. If a recipient's e-mail software can't read HTML-formatted mail, when the recipient displays the message, it is littered with HTML code, which can be annoying.

Microsoft Outlook Rich Text is a good option for people who correspond with individuals with older graphical e-mail programs because it allows you to add some simple formatting, and unlike HTML, Microsoft Outlook Rich Text–formatted messages can be read by many older e-mail programs. Plain Text, as its name conveys, is as simple as it gets. When you write messages in Plain Text format, none of the options on the Formatting toolbar are available. While this is a disadvantage, there is one big advantage to Plain Text–formatted messages—they translate well regardless of the recipient's Internet connection, e-mail software, or operating system.

## Message Header

The message header lists the **sender, recipient,** message **subject,** and a lot of other information. All you really need to know about the message header is this: if you right-click different parts of the message header, such as the sender name, you access a convenient shortcut menu of commands.

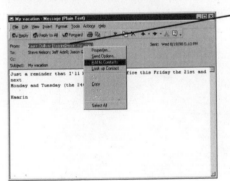

When you right-click one of the recipient names in the message header, Outlook displays a shortcut menu with a command for adding the person to your Contacts folder.

## Message Options

You can provide general instructions to Outlook concerning how to save, send, receive, and track messages. To specify these instructions in one fell swoop, choose the Tools menu's Options command, click the Preferences tab, and then click E-Mail Options. When Outlook displays the E-Mail Options dialog box, use the boxes and buttons to change the way e-mail messages are handled.

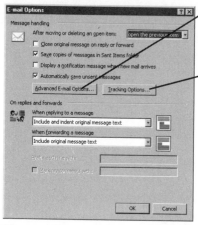

Click Advanced E-Mail Options to display a dialog box that lets you describe how Outlook saves, sends, and receives messages.

Click Tracking Options to display a dialog box that lets you specify how Outlook tracks messages sent over a local area network using an Exchange server.

You can also set options individually for each message as you write it. To do this, click the Options toolbar button in the Message form as you compose a message. Incidentally, if you've set mail options in the E-Mail Options dialog box, the settings you make for individual messages override the general ones.

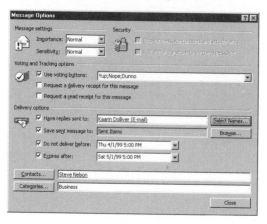

**SEE ALSO** Delivery Receipt; Importance; Read Receipt; Sensitivity

## Message Subject SEE Subject

## Microsoft Internet Explorer SEE Internet Explorer

## Microsoft Schedule+ SEE Schedule+

## Microsoft Word SEE Word

# MIME

MIME stands for "multipurpose Internet mail extensions." MIME is a protocol that lets you attach binary files to e-mail messages and send these over the Internet. As long as the people to whom you send messages also have e-mail readers that support the MIME protocol and the mail servers you and your recipients use support the MIME protocol, others can extract and use the files you send them. For example, using MIME, someone can attach a Microsoft Word document to an e-mail message. If the recipient's e-mail reader supports MIME, the recipient can save the Word document in the e-mail message. If the recipient has a copy of Word for Windows, they can open and work with the document in Word.

While Outlook understands and supports the MIME protocol, not all e-mail clients and servers do. For this reason, sometimes you can't use MIME. Sometimes you need to use Uuencode.

# My Documents

Windows supplies a folder, named My Documents, which it expects you'll use for storing many of the documents you create. Based on this assumption, Outlook's Open and Save As dialog boxes both provide a My Documents shortcut you can use to quickly open the My Documents folder.

# Net Folders

Net Folders allow you to share and synchronize any of your Outlook folders with other users across the Internet via special e-mail messages with embedded folder information. Net Folders come in handy for allowing others access to your Calendar or Contacts folders, or perhaps a special message folder you create.

To start using Net Folders, open the folder you want to share and then choose the File menu's Share command. Choose the submenu's This Folder command to start the Net Folders Wizard. Click Next, and then click Add to create a list of names of the people whom you want to allow access to your folder. Select names from your Address Book, and click To to add them to your list. Click OK when you're finished adding names, and then click Permissions to specify access privileges. Click Next, and then describe the folder in the text box. Click Next, and then click Finish.

# Netiquette SEE E-Mail Etiquette

# NetMeeting

Microsoft **Internet Explorer** and the full installation of Outlook come with a conferencing program called NetMeeting. NetMeeting lets you audio-conference or video-conference with another person over the Internet. To make full use of NetMeeting, you need speakers or headphones, a microphone, and optionally, a video camera.

### Using Outlook to Store NetMeeting Information

When you create contact items, you can enter NetMeeting information for the contact by clicking the Details tab of the Contact form. Enter the name of the directory server over which the Internet calls with the contact take place in the Directory Server text box. Enter the contact's e-mail alias in the E-Mail Alias text box.

To create a NetMeeting appointment in the Calendar, create an appointment item in the usual way and then select the This Is An Online Meeting check box. Select a server for the meeting location from the Directory Server drop-down list. Enter the e-mail address of the meeting organizer in the Organizer's E-Mail text box.

To organize an online meeting yourself and send meeting requests to other attendees, choose the Actions menu's New Meeting Request command.

### Starting NetMeeting

You can place a NetMeeting call to a contact by selecting the contact in your Contacts folder and choosing the Actions menu's Call Using NetMeeting command. You can place a NetMeeting call to someone on one of your other Address Book lists by choosing the Go menu's Internet Call command and the submenu's From Address Book command. You can also open NetMeeting by choosing the Go menu's Internet Call command.

**SEE ALSO    Plan A Meeting Wizard**

## Network

A network is just a group of computers that are hooked together so that the people who use the computers can share information. If you're using Outlook to send e-mail to coworkers, by the way, your computer probably is connected to a network.

**SEE ALSO    Internet; Intranet**

## Newsgroup  SEE  Newsreader

## Newsreader

Outlook 2000 comes with an Internet newsreader and a full-featured e-mail program called Outlook Express. Newsreaders let you read e-mail messages that people have posted to newsgroups. (A newsgroup works like an electronic bulletin board.) Using Outlook Express, you can also post your own messages to newsgroups.

### Installing Outlook Express

You install Outlook Express at the same time that you install Outlook. To configure Outlook Express so that it works with your **Internet service provider's** newsgroup server, you may need to run the Connection Wizard. Alternatively, you may need to get and then follow whatever configuration instructions your Internet service provider supplies.

### Starting Outlook Express

You can start Outlook Express from within Outlook by choosing the View menu's Go To command and then choosing News from the submenu.

*continues*

## Newsreader *(continued)*

### Previewing a Newsgroup

To check out the messages posted to a newsgroup, follow these steps:

**1** Select your news server from the Folders Pane.

**2** Click Newsgroups to display the Newsgroup Subscriptions dialog box.

**3** To display newsgroups on a certain topic, enter a keyword in the text box. Outlook Express lists all the newsgroups that include this keyword in their name.

**4** Select the newsgroup you want to preview, and then click Go To.

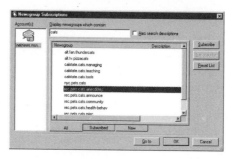

**5** To read a message, select one from the list. Outlook Express displays the message text in the Preview pane.

### Subscribing to a Newsgroup

To add a newsgroup to your newsgroup list so that you can easily visit the newsgroup on future occasions, you need to subscribe to the newsgroup. Subscribing doesn't cost you anything; it just allows you to access the newsgroup more quickly. To subscribe to a newsgroup you are previewing, right-click its name and choose the shortcut menu's Subscribe command. To subscribe to a newsgroup that isn't displayed in your newsgroup list, follow these steps:

**1** Select the server that stores the newsgroup from the list on the left.

**2** Click Newsgroups to display the list of newsgroups.

**3** Select the newsgroup to which you want to subscribe, and then click Subscribe.

### Unsubscribing from a Newsgroup

To unsubscribe from a newsgroup, click the server containing your subscribed newsgroup from the Folders pane on the left and then right-click the newsgroup from which you want to unsubscribe. Choose the shortcut menu's Unsubscribe option.

## Reading Messages

To read a message in a newsgroup, select the newsgroup in the Folder List pane. Outlook Express displays the message headers for the newsgroup's messages in the Message List pane. Click a message to display it in the Preview pane. If you double-click a message, Outlook Express displays the message in its own window.

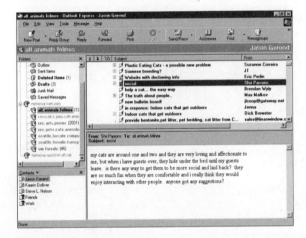

## Reading messages offline

The above procedure for reading messages works only if you are currently working online. For most people, staying online while working in Outlook Express is usually the easiest way to read newsgroup messages. However, with Outlook Express, you can also select the messages and headers you want to read, download them to your computer, and then read them offline.

### Reading an Attachment

Some messages include encoded attachments. Typically, you don't have to do anything special to read or save an attachment. If you open a message that includes a graphics image, for example, Outlook Express decodes the attachment and then displays the image in the Preview pane. If you open a message that includes another type of attachment—perhaps a program file, for example—Outlook Express decodes the attachment and then displays a shortcut icon for the file in the Preview pane. To save an attachment to your hard disk, right-click the image or its icon. Then choose the shortcut menu's Save As command.

*continues*

## Newsreader *(continued)*

## Stopping downloads of large messages

Large messages, such as those that include attachments, can take time to download. If you want to tell Outlook Express to stop downloading a message, click the Stop toolbar button.

### Working with Multipart Messages

Sometimes an attachment is too large to fit within a single message. When this is the case, the person posting the file splits the attachment across several messages, usually labeled something like 1 of 3, 2 of 3, and 3 of 3. To decode and then save an attachment that has been split across multiple messages, select the messages that hold the attachment. Then right-click the selection, and choose the shortcut menu's Combine And Decode command. When Outlook Express displays the Combine And Decode dialog box, click Move Up or Move Down to arrange the messages in the correct order. Then click OK.

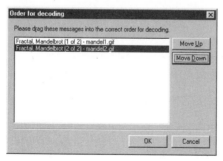

## Posting Messages

To post a message in a newsgroup, click the newsgroup item in the Folder List pane. Then click the New Message toolbar button. When Outlook Express displays a Message form, type your message and click Post.

## Posting Messages with Attachments

If you want to include an attachment with your message, click the Attach File toolbar button. (This button appears on the Message form's toolbar.) When Outlook Express displays the Insert Attachment dialog box, identify the folder that contains the file in the Look In drop-down list box. Double-click the file in the list box to attach it to the message.

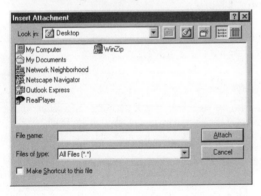

# Notes

Notes is one of the **Outlook folders,** and Notes themselves are just like, well, electronic sticky notes. You can use an Outlook Note to write down a phone number, an address, a quick to-do list—all the things you put on paper notes. As you can with the paper kind, you can stick one of these Notes on your desktop where it will serve as a reminder to you—until you get around to filing it more permanently or tossing it in the trash.

### Creating a Note

Creating a Note is simple. Just display the Notes folder, and click the New Note toolbar button. A blank Note pops up on your screen. Type the text you want to remember, click the Note's Close button, and you've created a Note.

Click the X to close a Note and add it to the Notes list.

### Customizing a Note

Click the icon in the Note's upper left corner to display the Note's Control menu. Choose the Control menu's Color command to change the Note's color. Choose **Categories** to assign the Note to a category.

### Working with Notes

Whenever you use the Taskbar to switch to another application, you usually hide any visible Notes. If you close or minimize all other applications, you can leave a Note on your desktop so you'll see it the next time you glance at your screen.

When you select something in a Note, you enable the Cut and Copy commands on the Control menu. Then you can paste part or all of the Note into a message or wherever else you want. You can paste the Clipboard's contents into a Note by choosing the Control menu's Paste command.

### Moving and Resizing a Note

To resize a Note, click and drag its edges as you would any other object. Click and drag the Note's title bar to move the Note anywhere on the screen.

### Keeping Track of Notes

To print a Note, choose the Control menu's Print command. Choose the Control menu's Save As command to save a Note to a folder anywhere on your hard disk. To forward a Note, choose the Control menu's **Forward** command. Outlook opens a Forward **Message form** so that you can send the Note anywhere you can send **e-mail.**

When you close a Note, it is automatically posted to the Notes folder. To view the Notes folder, click the Notes icon on the **Outlook Bar** or in the **Folder List.** You can **group** Notes as you would any other Outlook items. You can define **views** for the Notes list and use all the other **information viewer** features such as **sorting** and **filtering.**

### Deleting a Note

To delete a Note, select it in the Notes list and click the Delete toolbar button.

## Color-coding your Notes

By changing the color of Notes, you can code them. For example, make all of your phone number Notes yellow and all your reminders blue. Or use whatever combination you like. To change the color of a Note, right-click it in the Notes window, choose the shortcut menu's Color command, and then choose a color from the submenu.

## Office Assistant

Whenever you click the Office Assistant toolbar button or choose the Help menu's Microsoft Outlook Help command, an animated help guru called the Office Assistant pops up, assuming you have the Office Assistant installed. To use the Office Assistant, type your question in the box provided. Then click Search, and the Assistant displays a list of help topics that most closely relate to your question. To read a topic, click its button. When the Office Assistant has a tip for you, it displays a light-bulb icon. Click the light bulb to read the tip.

Type your question here.

## Offline Folders

An offline folder is a copy of the server folder that Outlook uses to actually deliver and store **messages.** If you use an offline folder—say you're not currently connected to the **network**—you periodically need to get it updated by **synchronizing** your files. First, however, you'll need to reconnect to the network.

**SEE ALSO**   **Remote Mail**

## Online Service SEE Internet Service Provider

## Organization

According to Outlook, an organization is a group of **Exchange serv**ers and Outlook clients that work happily together. In a little company, the organization might consist of a single server and half a dozen clients. In a big company, the organization might consist of dozens of servers and hundreds of clients scattered across multiple sites.

## Organize Pane

When you click the Organize toolbar button, Outlook opens the Organize pane. You can use the Organize pane to accomplish several tasks. You can use it to move items from one folder to another, to change the view of a folder, or to categorize items, for example. If you're looking at your Inbox folder and you click the Organize toolbar button, Outlook displays boxes and buttons that let you move messages to another message folder, use different colors for messages from different people, change your **view** of your Inbox, and create rules for handling **junk e-mail.** Other folders provide similar boxes and buttons for moving and rearranging their items.

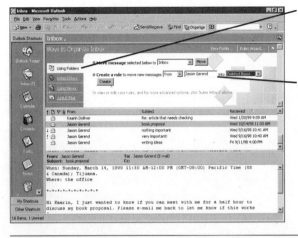

Click a hyperlink that describes how you want to organize the folder's items.

Describe how you want to organize the folder's items in these boxes.

## Using the Organize Pane to Move Items to Other Folders

You can use the Organize pane to move an item you specify to a folder you specify. If you choose to move the item to a different type of folder, Outlook automatically creates a new type of item for you. For example, if you choose to move a task from your Tasks list to your Calendar, Outlook creates a new appointment from the task. To use the Organize pane to move items, follow these steps:

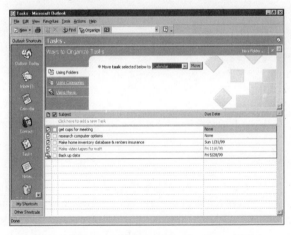

**1** Select the item you want to move to a different folder.

**2** Click the Using Folders tab.

*continues*

## Organize Pane (continued)

**3** Identify the folder you want to receive the new items by using the first drop-down list box. (The name of this list box differs depending on the folder you're in.)

**4** Click Move.

**5** In your Mail and Deleted Items folders, you have the option of creating a rule that moves all messages to or from the contact you specify to another folder.

### Using the Organize Pane to Create New Categories

You can also use the Organize pane to create new categories for items in your Calendar, Tasks, or Journal folders. To do this, select the item or items you want to categorize and then click the Organize toolbar button.

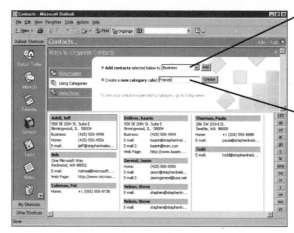

To add the selected item to an existing category, specify the category here and then click Add.

To create a new category for the selected item, enter it here and then click Create

**SEE ALSO    AutoCreate**

## Outlook Bar

The Outlook Bar lets you move around not only among the various Outlook folders but also around your entire computer and even your local network and the Internet. You can use the Outlook Bar and its shortcut icons in place of the Outlook Folder List to navigate within Outlook; furthermore, you can use it like Windows Explorer or My Computer to access any folder on your hard drive, other network drives, or on the Internet. And if there's a folder or web page you find yourself accessing frequently, you can place a shortcut to it on the Outlook Bar.

## Using the Outlook Bar to Navigate with Outlook

To move to an Outlook folder, click its icon on the Outlook Bar.

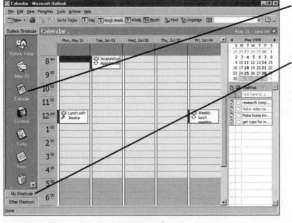

Click the
Calendar icon to
display the
Calendar.

Click My
Shortcuts to
display a group
of folders related
to e-mail.

## The Outlook Bar's Group buttons

If you used Outlook 97, you may have noticed that you don't have the Outlook Shortcuts, My
Shortcuts, and Other Shortcuts buttons on your Outlook Bar as described in this book. Your
buttons retained their names from the previous version of Outlook and are called Outlook,
Mail, and Other. While the names are a little different, the group of icons available when you
click one of these buttons is pretty much the same. That much said, if you get confused by the
explanations in this book and want to rename your Group buttons, just right-click a button
and choose the shortcut menu's Rename Group command. You can also create your own new
group by right-clicking the Outlook Bar and choosing the shortcut menu's Add New Group
command. Then add folder icons to the group by dragging them from the Folder List to the
Outlook Bar.

### Accessing My Computer, Other Folders, and the Internet Using the Outlook Bar

Click Other Shortcuts to display the My Computer, **My Documents**, and **Favorites**
shortcut icons. The Favorites folder contains the Internet addresses you've
selected as your favorites while browsing the **World Wide Web**. Just click an
icon to launch your **web browser** and the web page you selected.

*continues*

## Outlook Bar *(continued)*

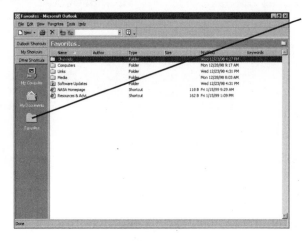

Click the
Favorites icon
to display the
contents of the
Favorites folder

### Customizing the Outlook Bar

To add an Outlook Bar shortcut icon that points to your favorite folder, follow
these steps:

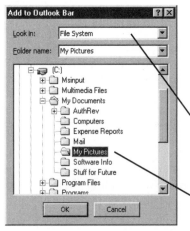

**1** Click the group on the Outlook Bar to
which you want to add the shortcut

**2** Right-click the Outlook Bar's back-
ground, and choose the shortcut
menu's Outlook Bar Shortcut
command.

**3** Choose whether you want to look in
Outlook or your computer's file
system for the folder by selecting an
entry from the Look In drop down list
box.

**4** Select the folder to which you want
to create a shortcut, and then click
OK.

### What's the big deal?

Why the fuss over the Outlook Bar when you can just use Windows Explorer to navigate the
folder hierarchy? Good question. You might not want to use the Outlook Bar in this manner.
However, if you're using Outlook to send and receive e-mail, check your schedule, and keep
track of your contacts, you'll probably be spending a lot of time there. And this means you
may find Outlook and its Outlook Bar much faster and more convenient than Windows
Explorer or the Start menu.

## Outlook Client

On a network, the messaging system really consists of two components: the Outlook client and the **Exchange server.** The Outlook client is a program that runs on your computer; the Exchange Server program runs on another computer. This Pocket Guide doesn't examine the server component of the messaging system except in passing. The server component of Outlook is the concern of the network administrator.

## Outlook Express

Microsoft **Internet Explorer** 5 comes with a "lite" version of Outlook called Outlook Express. So that's what Outlook Express is—a scaled-down version of Outlook. Unfortunately, there is a somewhat confusing twist to the relationship between Outlook and Outlook Express, which I'll mention because we're already on the subject. It turns out that Outlook Express comes with a **newsreader,** called Outlook Newsreader, which it shares with Outlook.

## Outlook Folders

This group of **folders** includes the Outlook Item folders: **Calendar, Contacts, Inbox, Journal, Notes,** and **Tasks.** You can open an Outlook folder by clicking its icon on the **Outlook Bar** or in the **Folder List.**

**SEE ALSO   Mail Folders**

## Outlook Item  SEE  Item

## Outlook Today

If you click the Outlook Today shortcut icon, Outlook displays a special, summary view of the items stored in your folders. This summary view lists new e-mail messages you've received, Calendar appointments or events you've scheduled for the current week, and tasks you've indicated you want to finish for the current week. You can also put links to your favorite web pages directly in Outlook Today, making it a sort of "home base" for Outlook and the Internet.

*continues*

## Outlook Today *(continued)*

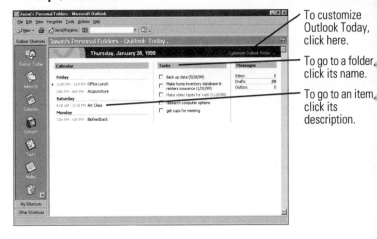

To customize Outlook Today, click here.

To go to a folder, click its name.

To go to an item, click its description.

## Out Of Office Assistant

If you're using the Corporate or Workgroup installation of Outlook, you can use the Out Of Office Assistant to automatically reply to **messages** that people send to you across an **Exchange Server.** In this way, you can let people know, for example, that you're on vacation for two weeks. Or you can let people know that you are in meetings all day and cannot respond to messages in a timely manner.

### Creating a Standard Response

To create a standard response that the Out Of Office Assistant can use to reply to every message you receive, choose the Tools menu's Out Of Office Assistant command. Outlook displays the Out Of Office Assistant dialog box.

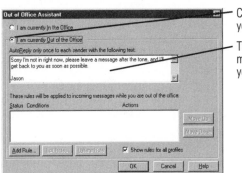

Click here to indicate that you're out of your office.

Type a standard reply to all messages that arrive while you're away.

## Using Rules and Actions

You may not want to handle all the incoming messages you receive when out of the office in the same way. If you want to be more specific, you can define rules that tell the Out Of Office Assistant how to monitor incoming messages and what to do when it sees a message you want processed in a certain way. To define rules such as these, follow these steps:

**1** Choose the Tools menu's Out Of Office Assistant command.

**2** Click Add Rule. Outlook displays the Edit Rule dialog box.

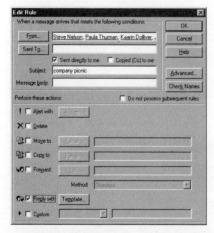

**3** Enter the sender name or recipient name whose messages you want the Out Of Office Assistant to look for, using semicolons to separate multiple names. (Click Check Names to verify the spelling of names.)

**4** Select the Sent Directly To Me or Copied (Cc) To Me check boxes to tell the Out Of Office Assistant to look for messages sent directly to you or only copied to you.

**5** Enter text in the Subject and Message Body boxes to tell the Out Of Office Assistant to look for messages that include specific words or phrases, using semicolons to separate words or phrases. Here, for example, I'm looking for messages relating to the upcoming company picnic.

**6** After defining the rules for monitoring your incoming messages, tell the Out Of Office Assistant what actions to take when it finds a message that meets the conditions described by your rules. To describe these rules, select the Edit Rule dialog box's Perform These Actions options, which are described in the table on the next page:

*continues*

## Out Of Office Assistant *(continued)*

| Action | Description |
|--------|-------------|
| Alert With | Out Of Office Assistant displays a pop-up message (with text you supply) or makes a sound. (Specify whether you want the pop-up message or the sound by clicking Action.) |
| Delete | Moves the message to your Deleted Items folder. |
| Move To | Moves the message to another **folder.** (Specify the folder by clicking Folder.) |
| Copy To | Makes a copy of the message, and places it in another folder. (Specify this other folder by clicking Folder.) |
| Forward | Forwards the message to another user. (Specify the user by entering a name in the text box.) |
| Reply With | Replies to the message with a standard response. (Specify the standard response by clicking Template to open a New Message form, and then type your response.) |
| Custom | Responds to the message with a customized response. (Ask the **administrator** about these.) |

After you define the rules and describe the actions that the Out Of Office Assistant should take when it sees a message that, according to your rules, is one you're interested in, click OK and the Out Of Office Assistant begins its work. Whenever you start the Out Of Office Assistant and it then sees an interesting message, it performs whatever action you specified. Click Move Up or Move Down in the Out Of Office Assistant dialog box to prioritize the rules and actions you specify.

### About the Advanced options

You can establish additional rules by clicking Advanced and using the Advanced dialog box's options. Its options let you tell the Out Of Office Assistant to look for messages with **attachments,** messages of a certain size, and messages that *don't* meet the conditions you specify. (Usually the Out Of Office Assistant looks for messages that do meet the conditions you specify.)

**SEE ALSO**  **Rules Wizard**

## PAB SEE **Personal Address Book**

## Panes

If you look closely at the right side of the Outlook window, you'll notice that it often provides several pieces of information about the items listed, depending upon the particular **Outlook folder** that's open. When the **Inbox** list is displayed, for example, icons identify messages that the **sender** flagged as important or that include an **attachment**. And the **information viewer** also identifies who sent the message and what its **subject** is.

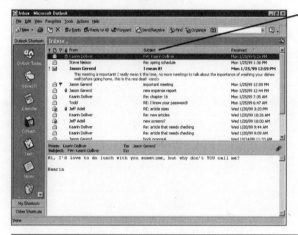

The Inbox information viewer provides several columns of information about messages.

### Editing View Columns

You can decide for yourself which information the Inbox displays in its information viewer. To do so, follow these steps:

**1** Choose the View menu's Current View command.

**2** Choose the submenu's Customize Current View command. Outlook displays the View Summary dialog box.

**3** Click Fields.

**4** Use the boxes and buttons in the Show Fields dialog box to add and remove message information.

*continues*

## Panes *(continued)*

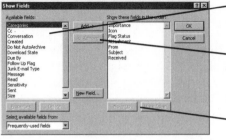

To add a field, select an entry in the Available Fields list box and then click Add.

To remove a field, select an entry in the Show These Fields In This Order list box and then click Remove.

To change the position of a column, click it and then click Move Up or Move Down.

### Different folders use different fields

The available fields in the Show Fields dialog box differ from one Outlook folder to another. In the **Calendar** folder, for example, available fields include Created, End, and Start. And in the Contacts folder, they include Job Title, Company, and Business Phone. You can change which fields you have available by selecting a different entry in the Select Available Fields From drop-down list box.

## Paragraph Alignment  SEE  Alignment

## Permission

Within an Exchange **organization,** the term *permission* refers to the ability to access items in a **Public Folder.** To read or place a **post** in a Public Folder, you must have permission. (The **administrator** gives permission.)

**SEE ALSO   Delegate Access**

## Personal Address Book

In Microsoft Exchange, you used a Personal Address Book to create a personal list of people's **e-mail names** (and a whole lot of other information as well). Because you may have used a previous Microsoft e-mail client, therefore, Outlook happily lets you work with Personal Address Books. In fact, in most cases when you add someone's name and e-mail address to the **Address Book,** for example, you actually get to choose whether that information goes into a Personal Address Book or the **Contacts** folder.

Don't confuse the Personal Address Book with the Address Book tool, by the way. The Address Book is a tool you use to view the contents of all the different places you store name and address information: a Personal Address Book, the Contacts folder, and if you're working on a network that includes an **Exchange server,** a Global Address List.

To view the contents of your Personal Address Book, click the Address Book toolbar button. When Outlook displays the Address Book window, select Personal Address Book in the Show Names From The list.

## Personal Folder

A Personal Folder is just a folder you use to store the items you create in Outlook and the messages you receive. Other users on your **network** can't read the messages in your Personal Folders unless you give them **delegate access** permission to do so.

**SEE ALSO    Public Folder; Synchronize**

## Plan A Meeting Wizard

Outlook's Plan A Meeting Wizard helps you schedule meetings. When you open your **Calendar** and choose the **Actions** menu's Plan A Meeting command, Outlook displays the Plan A Meeting dialog box. Outlook checks your schedule and the schedules of the prospective attendees and finds a time slot that appears as free time on everyone's schedule. If you're using the Corporate or Workgroup version of Outlook, the schedule information comes from the **Exchange server** or from published **iCalendar** files on the Internet; if you're using the Internet Only version of Outlook, the schedule information comes only from **iCalendar** files on the Internet.

### Planning a Meeting

To schedule a meeting from the Calendar folder, choose the Actions menu's Plan A Meeting command. Outlook displays the Plan A Meeting dialog box. Your name appears on the first line of the All Attendees list. Choose the day of the meeting by clicking a date in the Meeting Start Time drop-down calendar. Pick a tentative meeting time and duration by dragging the green and red selection bars.

*continues*

## Plan A Meeting Wizard *(continued)*

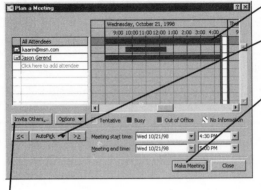

Busy times show up in blue on this schedule.

Click AutoPick to find the next available time slot that's free for all attendees.

Click Make Meeting to add the meeting to your Calendar and to send invitations (in the form of e-mail messages) to the prospective attendees.

To add an attendee, click Invite Others and select people from your Address Book.

**SEE ALSO**    **Calendar; NetMeeting**

---

# Pocket Outlook

Microsoft sells a special version of Outlook called Pocket Outlook for palmtop computers that use Windows CE. If you use Pocket Outlook, you can synchronize and share Pocket Outlook's information with Outlook's information. (This means, for example, that you can use Pocket Outlook when you travel and use Outlook in your office.)

---

# Post

A post is a special type of **message** that doesn't get delivered to a **recipient,** but gets delivered to a **Public Folder** on an **Exchange server.** In effect, posts are very much like the announcements tacked on the bulletin board at the local grocery store. You know the type I mean: the ones that advertise 13-year-old baby-sitters, '69 Camaros, and rewards for lost Labradors.

Posts are a slick way to share information with other Outlook **users** without having to send everybody an individual message. By having a Public Folder that stores, for example, one copy of a company's holiday schedule, holiday information is always available to everybody and is easy to get.

## Creating a Public Folder for Posting Information

To create a Public Folder for posts, select the Public Folders folder, choose the File menu's New command, and then choose the submenu's Folder command. When Outlook displays the Create New Folder dialog box, name the new folder, identify its contents, specify its location in the folder hierarchy, describe it briefly, and click OK. (You must have **permission** to do this.)

## Writing a Post

To write a post, select the Public Folder to which you want to post the information. Then click the New Post In This Folder toolbar button. When you click this button, Outlook probably displays an Untitled Discussion form that resembles the Message form. But if the person who created the Public Folder intends for you to use a different form for posts in the folder, the form you see might look a little different. For example, the folder creator might have designed a custom form for posts in that folder or might have told Outlook to use a different Outlook form, such as the Contact form, for posts in the folder. To select a different form for your post, choose the Tools menu's Forms command and the submenu's Choose Form command. To post a message using the Discussion form, follow these steps:

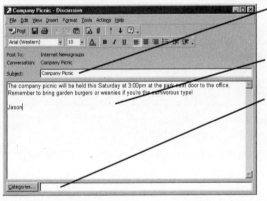

**1** Describe your message in a word or two.

**2** Type your message text here.

**3** Assign your message to a category and to send invitations (in the form of e-mail messages) to the prospective attendees.

## Attaching Outlook Items to a Post

You can attach any Outlook **item** to a post. To do this, choose the Insert menu's Item command. When Outlook displays the Insert Item dialog box, identify the item you want to send.

*continues*

## Post *(continued)*

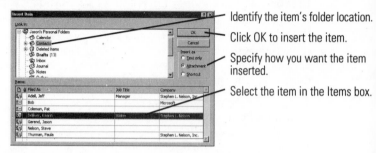

Identify the item's folder location.

Click OK to insert the item.

Specify how you want the item inserted.

Select the item in the Items box.

### Sending a Post

After you write a post, send it by clicking the Post toolbar button. Outlook places your post in the folder you selected.

### Posting a File

You can attach a file to a post in the same way you attach a file to any other Outlook item. You do this by clicking the Insert File toolbar button or by choosing the Insert menu's File command. But an easier way of sharing files in Public Folders is by posting the files on their own. This way they don't get lost or overlooked in messages. To post a file to a Public Folder, just click Other Shortcuts on the Outlook Bar and then click My Computer to locate the file you want to post. When you find the file, drag it to the Public Folder icon on the Outlook Bar or in your **Folder List.**

### Reading a Post

To read a post in a Public Folder, display the folder's contents list by clicking the folder's icon in the Folder List. Outlook lists any posts in the folder. To view a post, double-click it. When you do this, Outlook displays the post.

## Group post messages by conversation topic

The easiest way to review posts that were created in response to an original post is to group them by **conversation thread.** To do this, display the folder with the posts you want to view, choose the View menu's Current View command, and then choose the submenu's By Conversation Topic command.

## Replying to a Post

You can reply to a post in either of two ways: by replying directly to the post sender or by sending another post.

To reply directly to the sender, click the Reply toolbar button. Outlook opens a New Message form that contains a copy of the original post. Type your reply, and click the Send toolbar button.

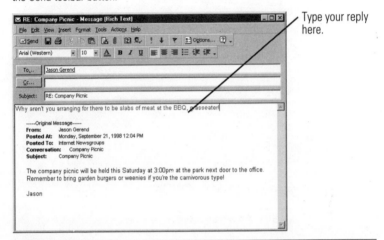

Type your reply here.

## Forwarding a Post

If you read a post that you want to forward to someone else, you can easily do so. First either select the post in the **information viewer** or display the post in its own window. Next click the Forward toolbar button. Outlook opens a New Message form that contains a copy of the original post.

Specify to whom you want to forward the post by entering an **e-mail name.**

## Printing a Post

You can print a post in the same way you print other Outlook items. First display the post. Then click the Print toolbar button.

If you want more control over how your post is printed, you can also choose the File menu's Print command. When Outlook displays the Print dialog box, choose a printer, specify the number of printed copies, describe what Outlook should do about any **attachments,** and so forth.

## Preview Pane

Outlook shows a Preview pane when you're viewing your Inbox folder. The Preview pane shows a portion of the selected message item.

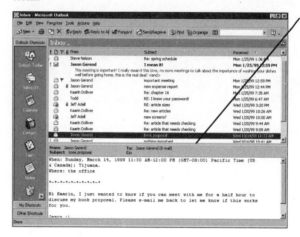

To change the size of the Preview pane, drag this bar.

**SEE ALSO** AutoPreview

## Priority SEE Importance

## Private Appointments and Tasks

You can mark an **appointment** or **task** as private either when you create the appointment or task or later on, after you've created it. Making an appointment or task "private" so that others don't know about it may seem sort of odd, until you remember that other **users** may be able to view your Calendar if you have given them **delegate access** permission. For example, you may not want your coworkers to know that you are visiting a doctor or that you are involved in a confidential meeting.

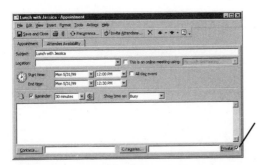

Select this check box to make an appointment private.

After you've marked a task or appointment as private, your co-workers can't see its details, all they see is that the time is busy, even if they have **permission** to view your **Calendar** and Tasks list.

## Viewing Other Outlook Users' Calendars

If you want to know what your coworkers' schedules look like, you must get delegate access to view their Calendars. Once you've done so, choose the File menu's Open command and the submenu's Other User's Folder command. Click Name, and select a name in the list in the Select Names dialog box. Click OK. Then select Calendar in the Folder drop-down list box, and click OK again. Outlook displays the Calendar of the person whose name you indicated.

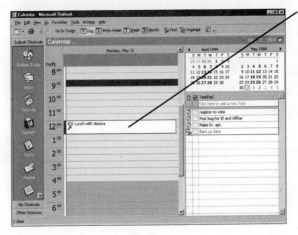

This is what an appointment looks like to you after you select the Private check box.

*continues*

## Private Appointments and Tasks *(continued)*

### Private text in your own schedule isn't hidden from you

The private text in your own Calendar and Tasks list isn't hidden from you. If you select an appointment or task, Outlook displays the appointment or task description.

## Private Folder  SEE  Personal Folder

## Profile

A profile lists the **information services** that an **e-mail client** such as Outlook knows how to use. You typically don't need to worry about profiles, however. The Outlook Setup program creates a profile for you when it installs the Outlook program by looking at the information services that you or your organization's administrator has already installed on your computer.

## Program

In this book, I use the term *program* to refer to software applications such as Outlook. I should note that technical types call these things "applications." My thought, however, is that any piece of software that you start by making a choice from the Programs menu in Windows is, in fact, a program.

## Program Window

In this book, the term *program window* refers to the window that appears when you start a **program**. Calling them program windows is not entirely kosher, however. Traditionally, these windows have been called application windows. But I think program window is a better term because Windows (and most nontechnical people) refer to software products such as Outlook as programs.

## Public Folder

Public Folders are the folders where you store **posts** and **files** that you want to make available to many people. Typically, you store posts in a Public Folder so you don't have to waste time sending a lot of people the same e-mail **message**.

## Read and Unread Messages

Both read and unread **messages** can be found in the **Inbox** or any other message folder (if you move them there or set up rules so that they go there instead of into the Inbox). To help you know which is which, Outlook displays unread message information in boldface characters and read message information in regular characters. Take a look at the figure to see what I mean.

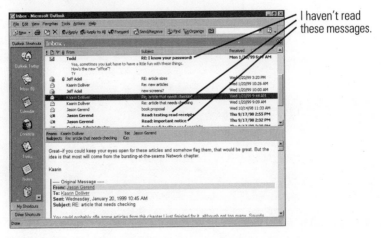

I haven't read these messages.

By the way, the Edit menu provides several commands for marking and unmarking read and unread messages. To use one of these commands, simply select the message you want to mark or unmark and then choose the command.

**SEE ALSO    Quick Reference: Edit Menu Commands**

## Read Receipt

Do you work with people who mysteriously lose or never receive the e-mail **messages** you send them? Read receipts are made for such occasions. While a **delivery receipt** confirms that a message got to a user's **Mailbox**, a read receipt confirms that a **user** has actually opened the message. If you're using the Corporate or Workgroup version of Outlook and you want to ask the **Exchange server** to confirm that a message has been opened, click the Options toolbar button in the Message form and then select the Tell Me When This Message Has Been Read check box under Voting And Tracking Options. However, if you are using the Internet Only version of Outlook, the recipient of your message receives a dialog box asking permission to send a read receipt back to the sender. In this way the recipient could hide the fact that they read the message.

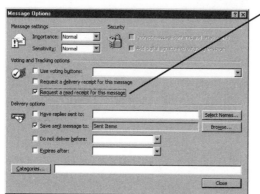

Select the Request A Read Receipt For This Message check box to ask the Exchange server to tell you when the message has been opened.

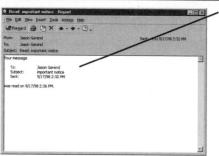

This is the type of message you receive, confirming that your message was opened.

## A word of warning

Read receipts and delivery receipts appear to be the perfect tools in **organizations** where paranoia and backbiting run rampant. Unfortunately, however, they triple the workload of your server because every message you create can trigger the creation of two more messages from the server (the delivery receipt message and the read receipt message). And these extra messages slow down the system for everybody. I'm not going to tell you how to run your department, but I will say that there are probably better ways to deal with your issues.

## Recipient

A recipient is any person who receives an e-mail message, whether it is a forwarded message, a reply, a meeting request, or otherwise.

**SEE ALSO   Sender**

## Recurring Appointment

You can create what's called a recurring appointment. In effect, this is an **appointment** that you want Outlook to schedule at a recurring interval: every day at 11:00 AM, every Friday at 5:00 PM, and so on. To create a recurring appointment, display the **Calendar** folder and then choose the Actions menu's New Recurring Appointment command. When Outlook displays the Appointment Recurrence dialog box, describe the appointment and how often it recurs.

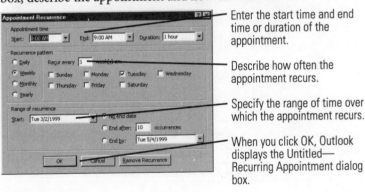

Enter the start time and end time or duration of the appointment.

Describe how often the appointment recurs.

Specify the range of time over which the appointment recurs.

When you click OK, Outlook displays the Untitled—Recurring Appointment dialog box.

*continues*

## Recurring Appointment *(continued)*

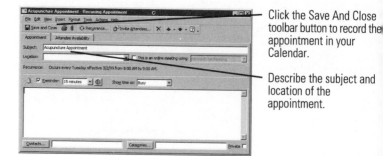

Click the Save And Close toolbar button to record the appointment in your Calendar.

Describe the subject and location of the appointment.

### Making an existing appointment recurring

If you want to make an existing appointment a recurring appointment, double-click the appointment to display its Appointment dialog box. Then click the Recurrence toolbar button and use the Appointment Recurrence dialog box to describe how often the appointment recurs.

**SEE ALSO** Recurring Task

## Recurring Task

You can tell Outlook to place a recurring **task** on your Tasks list. For example, if you prepare a report every Friday afternoon, you can add the "Do report" task to every Friday's Tasks list.

To create a recurring task, display your Tasks folder and click the New Task toolbar button. When Outlook displays the Task dialog box, use its boxes, buttons, and tabs to describe the task.

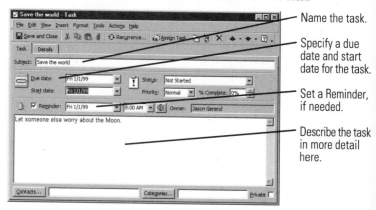

Name the task.

Specify a due date and start date for the task.

Set a Reminder, if needed.

Describe the task in more detail here.

When you finish describing the task using the Task dialog box, click the Recurrence toolbar button. Outlook displays the Task Recurrence dialog box.

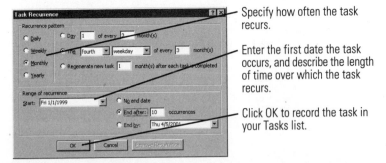

Specify how often the task recurs.

Enter the first date the task occurs, and describe the length of time over which the task recurs.

Click OK to record the task in your Tasks list.

## Making an existing task recurring

If you want to make an existing task recurring, double-click it to display its Task dialog box. When you click the Recurrence toolbar button, Outlook displays the Task Recurrence dialog box. You can use it to describe how often the task recurs.

**SEE ALSO    Recurring Appointment**

# Reminder

If you want to be reminded about an upcoming **task** or **appointment**, double-click the task or appointment and then select the Reminder check box in the dialog box. Outlook identifies the appointments and tasks it will remind you about with a little bell icon.

*continues*

## Reminder *(continued)*

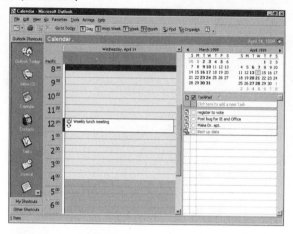

**SEE ALSO    Outlook Today**

## Remote Mail

Remote Mail is a useful tool for retrieving your e-mail while you're out of town and using another computer. Remote Mail lets you download only **message headers** and then choose from the headers which **messages** you want to download and read in their entirety. This can save you time and money if the computer you use on the road has a slower modem or if you must use a pay phone or make a long-distance connection. Remote Mail also lets you download copies of the messages you receive while you're away and leave the original messages on the server. This means that when you return to the office, you can download the messages again to have copies of them in your Inbox at work. You don't need to go through the tedious process of copying the messages from the computer you used on the road to your desktop at work. To use Remote Mail, you must first set up Remote Mail on the computer you use on the road. This means making sure you have a **Personal Folder** file on your computer, making sure that you have designated the Personal Folder file as a delivery location for your messages, and setting up your delivery service for use with Remote Mail. Once you have done this, you can use Remote Mail by choosing the Tools menu's Remote Mail command and then choosing a command from the submenu.

## Using offline folders

If your network uses Microsoft **Exchange Server,** you have the option of using **offline fold-ers** instead of, or in addition to, Remote Mail to make a remote connection. Offline folders give you several advantages over Remote Mail, including the ability to work with all of your Outlook folders, not just the Inbox.

**SEE ALSO   Synchronize**

## Reply

You can respond to a **message** you receive with a new, or reply, message. To do this, select or display the message to which you want to respond and then click either the Reply or the Reply To All toolbar button. The Reply button addresses your reply to only the message sender. The Reply To All button addresses your reply to any other message recipients as well as the sender. Outlook opens the **Message form,** which you use to create your response.

## Rules Wizard

The Rules Wizard helps you set rules that determine actions that Outlook will take automatically when certain conditions are met. For example, you can use the Rules Wizard to define an "important message" and then tell Outlook to notify you when an important message arrives by displaying a special pop-up announcement.

### Using the Rules Wizard to Create a New Rule

To use the Rules Wizard to create a new rule, choose the Tools menu's Rules Wizard command. When Outlook displays the first Rules Wizard dialog box, click New. Then follow the steps on the next page:

*continues*

## Rules Wizard *(continued)*

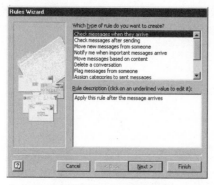

**1** In the first Rules Wizard dialog box, select the type of rule you want to create in the Which Type Of Rule Do You Want To Create list box. Then click Next.

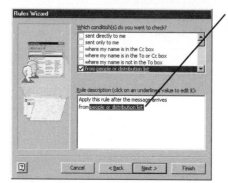

Click underlined words to fill in additional information.

**2** In the second Rules Wizard dialog box, select the condition(s) you want Outlook to watch for. Then click Next.

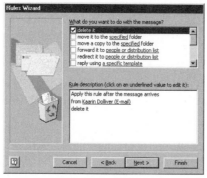

**3** In the third Rules Wizard dialog box, select the actions you want Outlook to take when the condition(s) you set are met. Then click Next.

**4** In the fourth Rules Wizard dialog box, select any exceptions to the rule. Then click Next.

**5** In the final Rules Wizard dialog box, name the rule, select the Turn On This Rule check box, and click Finish.

## Customizing rules

In any of the Rules Wizard dialog boxes, just click any underlined text in the Rule Description box to customize that text. For example, clicking people or distribution list will open a list of your Contacts so that you can choose people relevant to the rule you're creating.

### Using the Rules Wizard to Apply an Existing Rule

After you've created a rule, you can apply (or disable) any rule by choosing the Tools menu's Rules Wizard command. When Outlook displays the first Rules Wizard dialog box, apply or disable rules by selecting or clearing check boxes. To change the order in which rules are applied, click Move Up or Move Down.

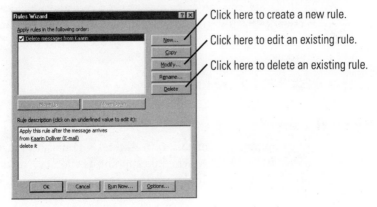

Click here to create a new rule.

Click here to edit an existing rule.

Click here to delete an existing rule.

**SEE ALSO**    **Out Of Office Assistant**

## Schedule+

Microsoft Schedule+ is another time-management component of the Exchange family of products. Using Schedule+, you can schedule appointments and meetings, keep a to-do list, and organize projects. Because you can do all these things in Outlook as well, you don't need Schedule+. But you should know that if you used Schedule+ with Exchange and you're hooked on it, you can still use it as your main scheduling program. To do this, choose the Tools menu's Options command, click the Preferences tab, click Calendar Options, and then select the Use Microsoft Schedule+ As My Primary Calendar check box.

## Sealed Message

As long as the **Exchange server** is configured the right way and Advanced Security is set up on the sender's and the recipient's Outlook clients, you can seal a **message** you've sent over a local area network. If you've signed up for a **digital ID** with a third-party verification service, you can also seal messages you send over the Internet.

**SEE ALSO**   Encryption; Security

## Second Time Zone

As an author, I often work with editors and publishers in other time zones. It is difficult to schedule **appointment** times with these people. You might think I could just add or subtract hours from my time, but that doesn't work. Some locations observe daylight saving time; others don't. And then, at least for me, things get really tricky when I'm working with someone on the other side of the International Date Line.

### How a Second Time Zone Helps

Thankfully, Outlook provides a feature for straightening out these time considerations: you can add a second time zone's information to your daily **Calendar.** In this way, it's easy to describe an appointment by using times either in your time zone or that of the person with whom you are communicating.

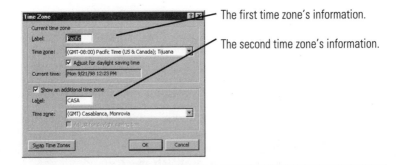

The first time zone's information.

The second time zone's information.

## Adding a Second Time Zone

To add a second time zone, choose the Tools menu's Options command, click the Preferences tab, click Calendar Options, and then click Time Zone. Select the Show An Additional Time Zone check box to add a second set of appointment times to your daily Calendar. To describe the second time zone, use the buttons and boxes of the Time Zone dialog box.

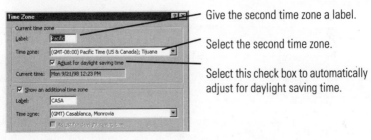

Give the second time zone a label.

Select the second time zone.

Select this check box to automatically adjust for daylight saving time.

# Security

Outlook provides different tools to make **e-mail** communications more secure. You can, for example, add digitally signed **messages** so that **recipients** and readers can be sure who messages came from and be sure as well that messages weren't tampered with. You can also encrypt messages so that recipients who don't know the encryption code can't read them.

To use any of these security tools on a network that includes an **Exchange server**, the security features must be installed on the **server** and enabled for the sender's **client** and all the recipients' clients. To use any of these security tools for Internet mail, you need to have a **digital ID**.

## Security Zones

You can designate a security zone for incoming HTML messages to tell Outlook how much protection you want from running scripts in HTML messages that could damage files on your computer. Outlook's initial security zone settings already provide a high level of security, so you probably don't want to adjust the settings unless you first learn more about how security zones work (such as by reading the online documentation). To designate a security zone for incoming HTML messages, choose the Tools menu's Options command, click the Security tab, and then select a zone in the Zone drop-down list box. If you want to change the level of trust for the zone you choose, click Zone Settings. Note that if you change a zone's settings, the new settings apply to Microsoft Internet Explorer as well.

## Sender

The sender is the person who creates and distributes a **message.** If I jot off a quick message to you suggesting lunch next Friday, for example, I'm the sender. You are the **recipient.**

## Sensitivity

You can assign different levels of sensitivity to **messages.** By doing so, **recipients** can tell whether they might want to be alone when they read the message. To assign a sensitivity level to a message, click the Options toolbar button in the **Message form.** Then use the Sensitivity drop-down list box to select a sensitivity level: Normal, Personal, Private, or Confidential.

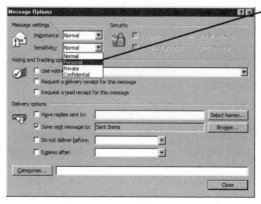

Message sensitivity information appears in the Sensitivity column of the information viewer, if that column is displayed.

## How sensitivity affects messages

For the most part, message sensitivity doesn't affect anything. All it does is help recipients tell what kind of messages they've been sent. However, the Private sensitivity level is slightly different from the other three in that private messages, when they are forwarded or replied to, can't be edited. In other words, if you mark messages as private, the recipients can still **forward** or **reply** to them. But Outlook doesn't let recipients change private messages when they forward or reply to them.

## Server

In most **networks,** there are two kinds of computers: **clients** and servers. A client is what sits on top of or alongside people's desks. A server is what sits in the computer room or over in the corner of the office. The relationship between a client and a server is very much like the relationship between a diner and a waiter. The diner continually bugs the waiter with requests: "Cheese omelet," "More coffee," "Check please." On a computer network, the requests made by the client to the server are a little bit different: "Save this file," "Print this report," "Distribute these e-mail messages." But the process is very similar in both situations. The server's job is to quickly and efficiently respond to all of the questions and requests from each of the clients being served.

If your computer is part of a network, much of the software you use has both a client and a server component. Take, for example, the case of Outlook. The windows, **forms,** and dialog boxes that you see on your computer screen are displayed and controlled by the **Outlook client,** which is the software **program** running on your computer. The program that does the dirty work of passing **messages** around the network is actually Microsoft **Exchange Server,** which is the software program running on the server computer.

## Server Extensions

Server extensions are small programs that run on a web server, enabling web publishers to easily upload files and run simple **server**-side programs in their **web pages** without having to write scripts.

There are two types of server extension that you need to know about: Microsoft FrontPage Server Extensions and Microsoft Office Server Extensions. FrontPage Server Extensions are useful to

*continues*

## Server Extensions *(continued)*

Outlook users who want to publish their **Calendars** or their free/busy information to the Internet as a web page because they make the process of publishing the files to the web server very easy. Office Server Extensions have all the same features that FrontPage Server Extensions do, but also add collaboration features that are useful to corporate users who need to work on a document with others across the Internet or an **intranet**.

**SEE ALSO   Busy Time**

## Service  SEE  Information Service

## Shortcut Icons

In general, shortcut icons on the **Outlook Bar** are divided into three groups: Outlook Shortcuts icons, My Shortcuts icons, and Other Shortcuts icons. The Outlook Shortcuts group includes shortcut icons that point to the standard Outlook folders, including the various Outlook **item** folders—**Inbox, Calendar, Contacts, Tasks, Journal,** and **Notes,** along with Deleted Items. The My Shortcuts icons point to a handful of special folders for dealing with Outlook's e-mail functions, including **Drafts,** Outbox, and Sent Items. The Other Shortcuts group provides icons that point to the My Computer folder, the **My Documents** folder, the **Favorites folder,** and any Public Folders you have on your network. Note that if you have upgraded from Outlook 97, however, your groups of shortcuts may be named Outlook, Mail, and Other. But these groups contain pretty much the same shortcut icons as the groups I have just described.

## Signature

For years now, people—particularly Internet **users**—have been appending little snippets of text called signatures to the ends of their **e-mail messages.** Sometimes signatures list the sender's name, address, and telephone number. But they can also include quotations, art, and even advanced **HTML** components. You can easily use Outlook to create a signature and append it to any message you want.

## Creating a Signature

To create a signature, choose the Tools menu's Options command and click the Mail Format tab. Then click Signature Picker. Click New in the Signature Picker dialog box to begin creating a new signature.

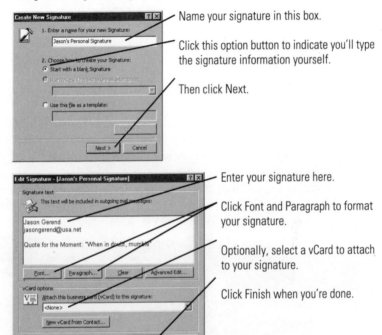

Name your signature in this box.

Click this option button to indicate you'll type the signature information yourself.

Then click Next.

Enter your signature here.

Click Font and Paragraph to format your signature.

Optionally, select a vCard to attach to your signature.

Click Finish when you're done.

If you don't want to use your new signature in all outgoing messages, select None in the Use This Signature By Default drop-down list box on the Mail Format tab of the Options dialog box.

## Using a Signature in a Single Message

To use a signature in a message, display the Message form and click the Signature toolbar button. Then choose the signature you want from the drop-down menu. If the signature you want isn't listed on the menu, choose More and then select the signature you want to use in the Select A Signature dialog box.

*continues*

## Signature *(continued)*

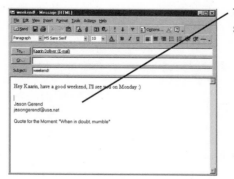

This block of text is the signature.

### Using an AutoSignature in All Your Messages

To use an AutoSignature in all your messages, display the Inbox folder and choose the Tools menu's Options command. When Outlook displays the Options dialog box, click the Mail Format tab. Then select the signature you want in the Use This Signature By Default drop-down list box.

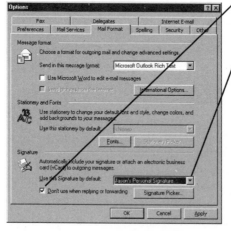

If you don't want to use a signature when replying to a message or forwarding a message, select this check box

If you don't want any signature by default, select None from this drop-down list box.

### Signature options

The amount of signature options you have depends on the **message format** you use. For example, if you use Plain Text, you can insert ASCII art but not image files. If you use HTML, you can use Microsoft FrontPage Express to create fancy HTML signatures. Note also that a signature you create in one format may not be available to messages written in another.

## Smiley

As a means of communication, e-mail has certain drawbacks. Even with really good writers (so I hear), it's easy for comments to be misinterpreted and for nuances to be lost. For these reasons, a lot of people use what are called smileys in their **messages.** A smiley is a combination of punctuation characters that, taken together, form a smiley face, a frowning face, or another kind of face.

You'll see smileys in your correspondence, so I'm not going to provide examples of them here. (They don't look all that great in books like this anyway.) Before I close this little digression, however, I want to mention what happens to smileys when you enter them with Microsoft **Word.** If Word is your e-mail editor—and there's a good chance it is—Word takes the smiley faces and frowning faces that you build with punctuation marks and replaces them with equivalent characters from the Wingdings dingbat font. (A dingbat font is just a font with a bunch of crazy characters.)

☺    This is what a smiley looks like when you use Word.

☹    This is what a frowning face looks like in Word.

## SMTP

SMTP is the acronym for Simple Mail Transfer Protocol. SMTP is the set of rules and conventions that Outlook uses to pass e-mail **messages** to the **Internet.** You see this acronym used a few places in Outlook, but you don't really need to know anything about it.

## Sorting

You can sort items in any Outlook **folder.** For example, Outlook lists **messages** in your **information viewer** in the order in which they were sent. But you can sort messages in other ways, for instance, by sender name or by message subject. To do this, choose the View menu's Current View command and then choose the submenu's Customize Current View command. When Outlook displays the View Summary dialog box, click Sort. To specify how you want messages sorted, select entries from the Sort Items By and Then By boxes and then click the Ascending or Descending option buttons.

*continues*

## Sorting *(continued)*

Specify how you want messages arranged in the Sort Items By drop-down list box.

## Spam

Spam refers to **junk e-mail.** While spam may seem innocuous at first blush, it actually represents a big problem. Let me explain. What happens with spam is that somebody who wants to sell something—lets say it's investment advice—builds a list of thousands and thousands of **e-mail addresses.** (Special spam mailing programs can do this by looking at the e-mail names and addresses of the people who **post** messages to newsgroups and by looking at online directories of e-mail names and addresses.) Once the spammer has this list, he or she begins sending huge volleys of junk e-mail messages to the names on the mailing list. The spammer may also sell the mailing list to other spammers. So quite shortly thousands and thousands of spammers are all sending thousands and thousands of junk e-mail messages.

This affects you personally in at least two ways. First, you may find your **Inbox** littered with junk e-mail messages (which causes all the same problems that junk snail-mail, also known as normal mail, causes). Second, the high volume of spam that's being passed around the Internet (on some mail **servers** spam accounts for 80 to 90 percent of the message volume) means that spam wastes bandwidth. When spammers fill up the bandwidth, all the rest of us have to take longer to send or receive messages or wait longer for web pages to download.

**SEE ALSO    Flame**

# Speed Dial

Speed Dial lets you create a list of phone numbers that you frequently call and then dial those numbers using your computer. (To use Speed Dial, you need to use the same telephone line for your modem and telephone.)

## Adding Numbers to the Speed Dial Menu

To add numbers to the Speed Dial menu, display the Contacts folder, choose the Actions menu's Call Contact command, and then choose the submenu's New Call command. When Outlook displays the New Call dialog box, click Dialing Options to display the Dialing Options dialog box.

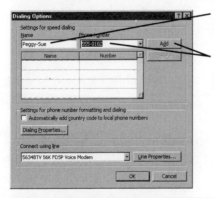

Type the name of the person you want to add to the Speed Dial list.

Type the phone number of the person you want to add to the Speed Dial list, and click Add.

## Using Speed Dial to Place a Call

To dial a number on the Speed Dial list, choose the Actions menu's Call Contact command and then choose the submenu's Speed Dial command. Choose the number you want to call from the Speed Dial submenu. In the New Call dialog box, click Start Call and then pick up the receiver after your computer and modem finish dialing the number.

When Outlook displays the Call Status dialog box, click Talk. When you complete your call, click Hang Up, replace the receiver, and click End Call in the Dial Phone dialog box. Then select another number in the Dial Number drop-down list, or if you have no other calls to make, click Close.

## Spelling Checker

You can—and you should—use Outlook's spelling checker to correct spelling errors in your e-mail **messages.** Misspelled words in messages make a bad impression. To check the spelling of the words in a message, choose the Tools menu's Spelling command. If Outlook finds a misspelled word, it displays the Spelling dialog box.

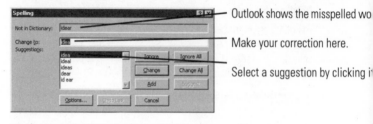

Outlook shows the misspelled wo

Make your correction here.

Select a suggestion by clicking i

### Spelling Buttons

The buttons in the Spelling dialog box assist in spell-checking and error-correction.

| Button | What it does |
| --- | --- |
| Ignore | Ignores only this occurrence of the word. |
| Ignore All | Ignores this and every other occurrence of the word. |
| Change | Changes this occurrence of the word to what the Change To box shows. |
| Change All | Changes this and every other occurrence of the word to what the Change To box shows. |
| Add | Adds the word to the spelling dictionary. |
| Suggest | Looks for similarly spelled words in the spelling dictionary. |

### Spelling Options

You can control, to a minor extent, the way in which Outlook's spelling checker works. To do this, choose the Tools menu's Options command and click the Spelling Tab. Or with the Spelling dialog box on your screen, click Options.

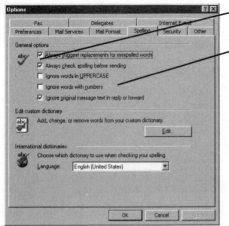

I recommend selecting both of these check boxes.

The Ignore options (the last three) let you weed out word and character strings that aren't going to appear in any dictionary—such as acronyms and alphanumeric codes. You can also tell Outlook to ignore the original text.

**SEE ALSO     Check Names**

## Startup Wizard

After you install the Outlook client, the first time you open Outlook the Startup Wizard is started to create your **profile.** The profile, in essence, lists which information services you will use with Outlook and describes how Outlook connects to these **information services.**

### Using the Startup Wizard

After installing Outlook, start Outlook by double-clicking its icon on the desktop or by clicking the Start button, choosing Programs, and then clicking the Outlook icon. To set up Outlook, follow these steps:

**1** Click Next to begin the setup process.

**2** If you are upgrading from an earlier version of Outlook and want to use your current Outlook settings, click Yes and click Next to open Outlook with your current settings. Otherwise, click No, and click Next.

*continues*

## Startup Wizard *(continued)*

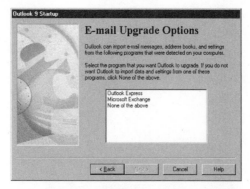

**3** If you are currently using a different e-mail client and want to import its set-tings, messages, and address books, select the client from the list of installed e-mail programs and click Next to complete the Startup Wizard. Otherwise, se-lect None Of The Above, and click Next.

**4** Select the type of e-mail service you want to use with Outlook, and click Next to finish the installation process. If you are prompted for a location for your Per-sonal Folders file, select the default or a subdirectory of the **My Documents** folder for easy backing up.

### About the different Outlook installation options

Outlook has three installation options: **Internet Only,** Corporate or Workgroup, and No E-Mail. Select the Internet Only option if you want to send and receive e-mail, but you don't need to access an **Exchange Server.** If you do need to access an Exchange Server, select the Corporate or Workgroup option. If you don't need any sort of e-mail service whatsoever and just want to use Outlook's advanced Calendar and contact management faculties, select the No E-Mail option. To switch the version of Outlook you're using, click the Tools menu's Op-tions command, click either the Mail Delivery or Mail Services tab, and then click Reconfigure Mail Support.

## Stationery

Outlook comes with various styles of stationery—message forms that use fancy HTML formatting to make your e-mail messages more colorful and interesting. To use HTML stationery, display the Inbox folder, choose the Actions menu's New Mail Message Using command, and then select a stationery, or choose More Stationery from the submenu. When Outlook displays the Select A Stationery dialog box, double-click the stationery you want to use.

To select a default stationery for all your outgoing messages, choose the Tools menu's Options command, click the Mail Format tab, and then select a stationery from the Use This Stationery By Default drop-down list box. Or you can click Stationery Picker, select a stationery, and then click OK.

**SEE ALSO    HTML Mail**

## Status Bar

The status bar appears along the bottom edge of the Outlook **program window** and tells you how many **items** are in the **folder** you selected. (If you don't see the status bar, choose the View menu's Status Bar command.)

The Outlook status bar counts the items in the selected folder.

## Subfolder

A subfolder is a folder within a folder. Using subfolders is a good way to organize your messages.

## Subject

When you create a **message,** you have the option of including a brief description of the message's subject. I recommend including meaningful subject descriptions with messages. They make it easier for people to **sort** and **filter** messages. By including a subject, you increase the chances of someone saving your message for future reference. And **recipients** will probably read your messages sooner.

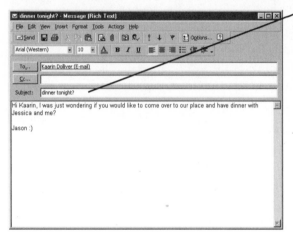

Here's where you enter the message subject. As soon as you do, Outlook renames the Message form using the subject.

## Synchronize

If you work with **offline folders,** you need to synchronize your online and offline folders when you log on to your network. When you synchronize your folders, any changes you make while using your folders offline are incorporated into your online folders so that sets of folders are identical. To synchronize folders, choose the Tools menu's Synchronize command and then choose the submenu's All Folders command.

### Save a Synchronization File for Another Computer

To save a synchronization file for synchronizing your Outlook folders with another computer's, choose the Tools menu's Synchronize Other Computer command and the submenu's Save File command. Click New to create a synchronization file for a computer you haven't synchronized before. Name the computer you're currently using, and then name the computer you're going to synchronize. Select the folders you want to synchronize, and then click OK.

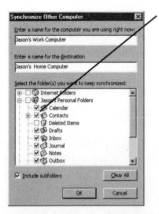

Choose the folders you want to keep synchronized by clicking the check boxes.

### Open a Synchronization File From Another Computer

To synchronize the Outlook folders on your computer with those on another computer from which you already created a synchronization file, choose the Tools menu's Synchronize Other Computer command and then choose the submenu's Open File command. Enter the location of the synchronization file in the text box provided, or click Browse. Choose how Outlook should deal with conflicts by clicking option buttons under Conflicting Items, and then click OK to begin synchronizing.

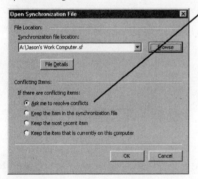

Choose to be prompted when there is a conflict.

**SEE ALSO    Remote Mail**

## Task Filters

Outlook lets you filter the tasks in the Tasks list so you can decide which tasks appear in the list. For example, you can show only tasks that you haven't yet finished, or tasks that you should have finished by now but haven't, or even tasks that you haven't yet started. To perform this filtering, choose the View menu's Current

*continues*

## Task Filters *(continued)*

View command and then choose the submenu's Customize Current View command. When Outlook displays the View Summary dialog box, click Filter.

**SEE ALSO**    Folder View

## Task List  SEE  Tasks

## TaskPad

The TaskPad is the small task list you see in the lower right corner of the **Calendar** folder. When you add a new task to the TaskPad, it shows up on the main Tasks list in the **Tasks** folder.

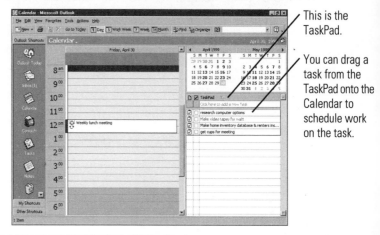

This is the TaskPad.

You can drag a task from the TaskPad onto the Calendar to schedule work on the task.

## Tasks

Outlook lets you build a list of the tasks you're supposed to do. You can organize tasks into projects by grouping them into **categories,** or you can **group** them by a variety of other criteria. You can **filter** tasks to display certain ones, **sort** tasks in the Tasks list, and drag tasks to move them up and down in the Tasks list. You can even assign tasks to your coworkers, track the progress you've made on completing tasks, and send reports to your colleagues describing the **task status.**

## Adding a Task to the Tasks List

To add a task to your Tasks list, click the Tasks icon on the **Outlook Bar.** Then click the top line of the Tasks list in the Subject **field** (where it says *Click here to add a new Task*).

To provide more information about a task you're adding, click the New Task toolbar button.

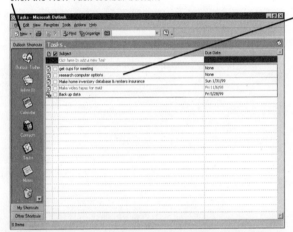

Type a short description of the task.

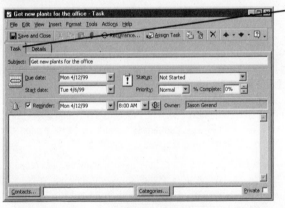

Use the tabs, buttons, and boxes in the Task window to describe the task in detail.

## Viewing the Tasks List

Outlook supplies 10 predefined **views** of the Tasks list, including Simple List, Detailed List, Active Tasks, Completed Tasks, and Task Timeline. To select which tasks appear, choose the View menu's Current View command.

*continues*

## Tasks *(continued)*

### Assigning a Task

If you have the authority, you can assign tasks to your coworkers using Outlook. Double-click an existing task on the Tasks list, or click the New Task toolbar button to open a new Task form. In the Task form, click the Assign Task toolbar button. Outlook displays an altered Task form.

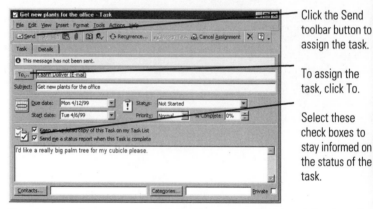

Click the Send toolbar button to assign the task.

To assign the task, click To.

Select these check boxes to stay informed on the status of the task.

The person to whom you assign the task can accept, decline, or reassign the task.

### Accepting, Declining, and Reassigning Tasks

If you are assigned a task, you can accept it by clicking Accept when you receive the message. When Outlook displays the Accepting Task dialog box, you can simply accept the task or you can accept it and add a comment. To accept a task without adding a comment, click the Send The Response Now option button and then click OK. To add a comment, click the Edit The Response Before Sending option button and then click OK. Type your response, and then click the Send toolbar button. When you accept a task, you become the "owner" of the task. You can decline a task the same way you accept one.

To reassign a task, open the message that contains the task request. Click Assign Task, and type the name of the person to whom you want to assign the task in the To box. Then click the Send toolbar button. The new task recipient then has the option of accepting, declining, or reassigning the task.

### Categorizing and Prioritizing Tasks

To assign a task to a **category,** click Categories and select a category from the list in the Categories dialog box or create a new category. Then click OK.

To prioritize a task, display the Priority drop-down list and select Normal, High, or Low priority from the list. High-priority tasks are marked with a red exclamation point in the Detailed List Task view.

**SEE ALSO   Recurring Task; Task Status**

## Task Status

You can track the status of a task you are working on and let other members of your workgroup know the task status. Tasks can be assigned the status Not Started, In Progress, Completed, Waiting On Someone Else, or Deferred. In addition, you can indicate the percent completion of a task and note the total and actual work done on a task.

### Tracking the Status of a Task

To display a task in your Tasks list, double-click it or click the New Task button to open a new Task form. Click the Task tab, select a status from the Status drop-down list, and use the % Complete spin box to indicate the percentage of the task already completed. Then click the Details tab.

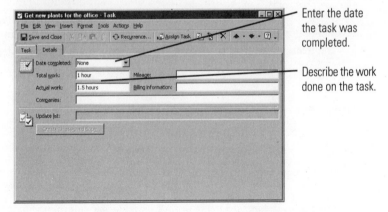

Enter the date the task was completed.

Describe the work done on the task.

*continues*

## Task Status *(continued)*

### Sending a Task Status Report

To send a task status report, double-click the task in the Tasks list. Choose the Actions menu's Send Status Report command. Outlook displays the Task Status Report—Message form.

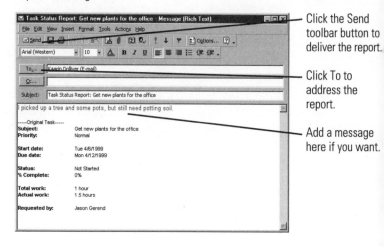

Click the Send toolbar button to deliver the report.

Click To to address the report.

Add a message here if you want.

## Tentative Appointment

A tentative appointment shows up in your appointment **Calendar,** but it isn't considered **busy time.** As a result, an **appointment** that you mark as tentative doesn't preclude the **Plan A Meeting Wizard** from scheduling a meeting for the same time as the tentative appointment.

## Thread SEE Conversation Thread

## Time Zone SEE Second Time Zone

## To-Do List

Outlook lets you keep an online to-do list, which it calls a **Tasks** list. With the list, you can keep track of the tasks you're supposed to do but haven't yet done.

**SEE ALSO** Reminder; TaskPad

# Toolbar

Outlook features toolbars to make things easier for you. (A toolbar is just a group of clickable buttons.) Because it's usually easier to click a button than choose a command, I emphasize the toolbar way in this little book. Like all the other programs in Microsoft Office, Outlook has menus that display toolbar-button icons next to menu commands to help you remember the association. By the way, if your **program window** doesn't show a toolbar, choose the View menu's Toolbars command and then choose one of the toolbars listed. You can then click the vertical bar on the left side of the toolbar to position it wherever you like.

## Outlook will customize your toolbars

If you have more than one toolbar displayed and you position them to be in one row, Outlook keeps track of which buttons you use the most and will rearrange the buttons to suit your usage patterns.

### Customize a Toolbar

Outlook 2000 lets you customize your toolbars, create your own custom toolbars, and it will also customize your toolbars based on the way you use them. To customize an existing toolbar, right-click the toolbar and choose the shortcut menu's Customize command. When Outlook displays the Customize dialog box, use the Commands tab to drag menu commands to the toolbar. To edit a toolbar button, display the Customize dialog box and then right-click the toolbar button. Use the shortcut menu to rename the button or change its options. To rearrange the buttons on a toolbar, display the Customize dialog box and then drag the buttons to new locations on the toolbar. To create a new toolbar, click New in the Customize dialog box.

**SEE ALSO    Adaptability; Quick Reference: Toolbar Buttons**

# Undo

You can typically undo your last editing change to a **message**. To do this, choose the Edit menu's Undo command.

# Unread Messages  SEE  Read and Unread Messages

# URL

A URL, short for uniform resource locator, specifies how you find an **Internet** resource such as a **World Wide Web** page. A URL has four parts: the service, or protocol; the server name; the path; and the document, or file, name.

---

### A Sample URL Explained

Let me explain the four parts of a URL by using a real-life **web page**—the cover page of the Internal Revenue Service's online newspaper called the *Digital Daily*. Here it is:

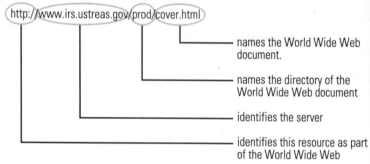

http://www.irs.ustreas.gov/prod/cover.html

names the World Wide Web document.

names the directory of the World Wide Web document

identifies the server

identifies this resource as part of the World Wide Web

**SEE ALSO    HTML; Hyperlink**

---

# Users

Users are the people who use Outlook. (In particular, they're the ones who use it as a network **client.**)

---

# Uuencode

Some e-mail systems (although thankfully not Outlook) don't let you include files in your e-mail **message.** With these systems, you can send only text.

Okay. I know what you're thinking. Not being able to attach a nontext file to an e-mail message seems like a pretty big limitation. And you're right. So to deal with this limitation, people created a **program** called Uuencode (pronounced you-you-en-code). It converts, or encodes, nontext files to text files so that they can be included in e-mail messages such as those sent over the Internet. At the other end, when the **recipient** gets the message, the program converts, or decodes, the text files and turns them back into nontext files.

Outlook takes care of encoding and decoding Internet e-mail **attachments** automatically. And unless you specify that you want to use Uuencode, Outlook uses a standard called MIME for e-mail attachments you send.

## vCalendar SEE iCalendar

## vCard

A vCard is a virtual business card you attach to Internet e-mail messages. You can exchange vCards in e-mail messages as a quick and easy way of distributing your contact information. When you receive a vCard from someone, you can save the vCard as a contact item by dragging the vCard to your **Contacts** folder, reviewing the new contact, and then clicking the Save And Close toolbar button. To create a vCard, display the Contacts folder, right-click the contact for whom you want to create a vCard, and then choose the shortcut menu's Export To vCard File command. When Outlook displays the Save As dialog box, make sure the Save As Type box says vCard files. To forward a contact as a vCard, select the contact and then choose the Actions menu's Forward As vCard command to open a new mail message with the vCard attached.

## Views

Each Outlook **folder** comes with several different views. A view organizes the **items** in a folder by specifying which **fields** appear, how items should be **grouped** or **sorted,** and whether any **filters** should be used. Outlook offers many types of views. Some view types are better suited for particular Outlook items.

*continues*

**Views** *(continued)*

### Choosing a View

To select a view, choose the View menu's Current View command. When Outlook displays the Current View submenu, select the view you want to use. Note that different Outlook folders offer different views.

### Modifying a Standard View

You can modify standard Outlook views to suit your preferences and needs. To do so, display a standard view, choose the View menu's Current View command, and then choose the submenu's Customize Current View command. When Outlook displays the View Summary dialog box, click a button to tell Outlook how you want to modify the view.

Click Fields to change the fields displayed in the view.

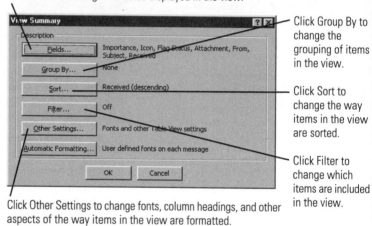

Click Group By to change the grouping of items in the view.

Click Sort to change the way items in the view are sorted.

Click Filter to change which items are included in the view.

Click Other Settings to change fonts, column headings, and other aspects of the way items in the view are formatted.

### Defining a New View

The standard views that Outlook initially provides may be the only ones you need. But you can easily create your own views. Choose the View menu's Current View command, and then choose the submenu's Define Views command. When Outlook displays the Define Views dialog box, click New. Outlook displays the Create A New View dialog box.

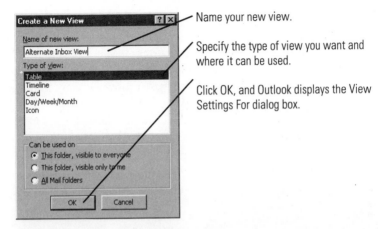

Name your new view.

Specify the type of view you want and where it can be used.

Click OK, and Outlook displays the View Settings For dialog box.

After naming the view, use the View Summary dialog box to specify the columns of message information, grouping, sorting, filtering, and formatting you want in your new view. Click OK when you're finished.

Click Apply View and Close in the Define Views dialog box to see your new view.

**SEE ALSO    Columns; Message Flag**

## Voting Buttons

You can put voting buttons on e-mail messages so that recipients can reply merely by clicking "Yes" or "No"; "Accept" or "Reject"; or "Yes," "No," or "Maybe." To create a democratic message, fill in the Message form and click the Options toolbar button. Then select the Use Voting Buttons check box, and select a set of voting buttons.

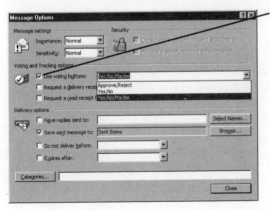

Select this check box to add voting buttons to a message, and then select a set of voting buttons.

## Web Browser

A web browser is a program that lets you look at World Wide Web documents. Netscape Navigator and Microsoft Internet Explorer (which comes with Windows and Outlook 2000) are both web browsers. Most browsers let you browse, or view, both the graphics and text components of World Wide Web documents, but there are also browsers that let you look at just the text. (You might want to do this, for example, if your connection to the Internet is slow—say, less than 14.4 Kbps—or if you really are interested in only the text portions of the documents you are viewing.)

**SEE ALSO   Web Page**

## Web Folders

The Web Folder shortcut icon, which appears in the Look In drop-down list box in the Save As dialog box, lists web server locations where you can publish Outlook information.

## Web Page

Web page is another name for a document on the **World Wide Web,** the most popular part of the **Internet.** Web pages often combine text, graphics, and other elements, including sound and video clips, and 3D worlds. Web pages also usually include **hyperlinks,** or jumps, to other web pages.

## WinFax Starter Edition SEE Fax

## Word

If you have Microsoft Word 2000, you can use Word as your e-mail editor and call on the power of Word to help you write your messages. To tell Outlook you want to use Word as your e-mail editor, choose the Tools menu's Options command. On the Mail Format tab, select the Use Microsoft Word To Edit E-mail Messages check box. The next time you open a new Message form, Outlook displays a little message box to alert you that it is opening Word as your e-mail editor. If you look carefully, you can see that the Message form now includes extra buttons on the toolbars. (You might recognize these buttons from Word.) You can use these buttons to edit and format your e-mail messages.

## Word Mail Merge

You can use the name and address information stored in your Outlook Contacts folder in a Microsoft Word mail merge. For information about how to do this, refer to your Word documentation.

## World Wide Web

The World Wide Web (also known as WWW or simply the Web) is a set of multimedia documents that are connected so you can jump from one document to another using **hyperlinks,** usually with just a mouse click. The multimedia part means that you're not limited to words: you can place pictures, sounds, and even video clips in a web document.

To view a WWW document, you need to have a **web browser.** Popular web browsers include Netscape Navigator and Microsoft Internet Explorer. If you want to start exploring the Web, try using a search tool such as Yahoo! You can find it at the following **URL:**

*http://www.yahoo.com*

It provides a directory of thousands of different World Wide Web sites.

## Zip

When people say a **file** is zipped, they usually mean it's been compressed using the PKZIP or WinZip utility. To use a zipped file, you have to unzip it.

Zipping a large file before you attach it to an e-mail message is a good idea—especially if you have the problems of limited disk space or slow transmission times.

# Troubleshooting

Got a problem? Starting on the next page are solutions to the problems that sometimes plague new users of Microsoft Outlook 2000. You'll be on your way—and safely out of trouble—in no time.

## Menus and Toolbars

**You Can't Find a Menu Command or Toolbar Button**

Outlook has a new feature: Personal Menus. When you first start working with the program, it keeps track of those menu commands you use and don't use, and it automatically customizes your menus. This feature is convenient because when the menus become shorter, you'll find it easier to access the commands you use most.

However, it can be a little disconcerting when commands just up and vanish.

### Find the missing commands

The hidden commands aren't really gone; they're just hiding. To use one of them, just hold your cursor on the menu title for a few seconds and the full list of commands will pop up.

If the full list of menu commands doesn't appear, choose the Tools menu's Customize command, click the Options tab, and make sure that the Show Full Menus After A Short Delay check box is selected.

### Reset your menus and toolbars

You can also reset your menus and toolbars to their original configuration by clicking Reset My Usage Data. Outlook will start learning your preferences all over again.

## E-Mail

**You Don't Know Someone's E-Mail Address**

You want to send so-and-so an e-mail **message**, but you don't have the address? Don't feel embarrassed. I think this is probably the most common e-mail problem of all. Fortunately, this problem is easy to solve.

**Check the Global Address List**

If the certain someone to whom you want to send a message is an Outlook **user** on your **network,** you can get the **e-mail name** from the **Global Address List.** To do this, click the Address Book toolbar button and follow these steps:

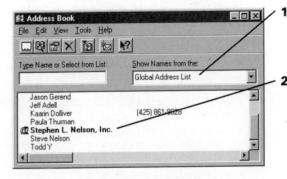

1 Select Global Address List in the Show Names From The drop-down list box.

2 Scroll through the list of names until you find the person to whom you want to send a message.

 **Call them and ask**

If someone isn't a user on your network but your Outlook system is connected to the **Internet,** you can still send the message. You just can't look up the missing address in your Global Address List. Your best bet is to call and ask for the correct e-mail name. Sounds silly, doesn't it? But this really is the best solution. So go and do it. Once you know this information, you just send your message to

*e-mailname@domainname*

For example, if you wanted to send an e-mail message to me, you would send the message to:

*steve@stephenlnelson.com*

My user name is *steve.* And *stephenlnelson.com* is the domain name.

*continues*

## You Don't Know Someone's E-Mail Address *(continued)*

### Ask them to e-mail you first

If you want to send someone e-mail but your real problem is that you're not familiar with this computerized, electronic mail thing, your best bet may be to get the other person to send you an e-mail message. (If you are on a network, you may need to ask your administrator for your e-mail name and domain name if the other person will be sending you e-mail over the Internet.) But if you provide this information to the person with whom you want to correspond and they are technically astute, it will be easy for the other person to send e-mail to you.

When you get the message—you'll see it in your **Inbox**—double-click it and read it. Then right-click the sender's name in the **message header,** and choose the shortcut menu's Add To Contacts command. What you've just done is added the sender's e-mail name (and all the other information you need to send them e-mail messages) to your **Contacts** list.

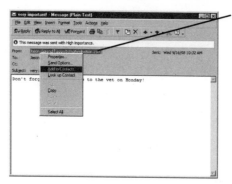

Right-click here to display the shortcut menu.

After you've added a person's name to your Contacts list, it's easy to address a message to the person. All you have to do is click To or Cc when you're writing the message so that Outlook displays the Select Names dialog box. Then follow these steps:

**1** Select Contacts in the Show Names From The list box.

**2** Scroll through the list of names until you find the person to whom you want to send a message.

**3** Double-click the person's name.

### Search directories on the Web

If you want to find a long-lost friend's e-mail address, try conducting an online search using a directory service. To do this, click the Start button, choose Find, and then choose People. Use the Look In drop-down list box to select the name of a directory service. (It doesn't really matter which one you choose first— you'll probably have to try several.) Then enter as much of the person's name as you can remember in the Name box, and click Find Now. The directory service lists all the names in its database that match the text you entered. If the directory service doesn't find a match, don't give up. Try another service, or try adding more or less information to the Name text box.

## Your Messages Aren't Getting Through

Occasionally, a message recipient might not receive a message you sent, even though you used the correct address. Here are a few ways you can help determine the cause of this problem and solve it.

### E-mail yourself a message to make sure your e-mail is working

Your first step should be to e-mail yourself a message. You can do this simply by naming yourself in the message as the recipient. The **Outlook client** delivers the message to the **Exchange server** or Internet mail server and then, assuming everything goes smoothly, the server delivers the message to your **Inbox**.

If you can't e-mail yourself a message, contact the network administrator. The problem isn't actually yours to worry about: it's the administrator's problem. (Do, however, make sure you are really e-mailing yourself and not somebody else with a similar name in another department.)

*continues*

## Your Messages Aren't Getting Through *(continued)*

### Request a return receipt or a read-notification receipt

If most of your messages reach their recipients but certain types don't seem to get through—or messages to certain recipients don't seem to get through—the problem might be one of human error. For example, Joe Bob in purchasing might have forgotten that he received messages from you. In cases like these, you can tell Outlook to alert you to the fact that, for example, Joe Bob has indeed received your message or that Joe Bob has indeed read your message. To do this, click the Options toolbar button when the **Message form** is displayed.

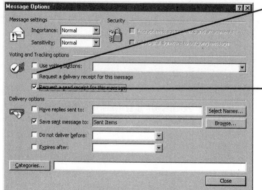

Select this tracking option to have the server acknowledge delivery of your message.

Select this tracking option to have the server monitor the recipient's Inbox and tell you when the recipient opened the message.

## You're Getting Too Many Messages

In **organizations** where everybody uses e-mail, it's easy to get overwhelmed with e-mail **messages.** Secretaries. Managers with lots of direct and indirect subordinates. People in service departments. The truth is short of an organizational e-mail policy that attempts to limit frivolous e-mail traffic, you can't do much to reduce the volume of incoming messages. But I do have three ideas for you if you're getting overloaded.

### Don't use read receipts or delivery notifications wantonly

Okay, I know I said earlier that **read receipts** and **delivery receipts** are useful, but they also clog up your **Inbox** with one or two extra messages for every message you send. So don't use them unless you have to.

### Don't needlessly reply to or forward messages

As sure as the sun rises in the east, the more messages you **reply** to and **forward**, the more you'll receive. The reason, of course, is that the recipient of a reply message or forwarded message generates another reply a certain percentage of the time. And this is true even if you shouldn't have created the reply message or forwarded the message in the first place.

I'm not suggesting that you stop replying to your boss's messages or that you not forward messages when appropriate. But you should be judicious. It's easy to reply to or forward messages, but it isn't always necessary.

 ### Use the Organize pane to filter messages

You can get Outlook's help when it comes to managing incoming messages. Just create a rule using the **Organize pane** or the **Rules Wizard** that tells Outlook to move certain messages to other folders or delete junk e-mail, as appropriate. To do this, click the Organize toolbar button in the Inbox.

## Are you getting junk mail?

If you're getting electronic mail from someone you'd rather not correspond with, you can use the Organize pane to automatically delete all messages you receive from that person. To do this, click the Organize pane's Junk E-Mail tab. Use this tab to name the joker who keeps sending you e-mail, and tell Outlook to delete any messages they send you.

## Your Folders Are Full

Folders can quickly overflow with **messages** if you regularly correspond via e-mail. Fortunately, it's easy to clean up a folder.

 ### Delete individual messages you don't need

To delete a message, select it and then click the Delete toolbar button. If you want to save a copy of a message, be sure to print it before you delete it.

*continues*

## Your Folders Are Full *(continued)*

### Empty the Deleted Items folder

You can delete all the messages in your Deleted Items folder by right-clicking the Deleted Items folder and choosing the shortcut menu's Empty "Deleted Items" Folder command. It's a good idea to regularly remove the messages in the Deleted Items folder. (When you delete a message in the **Inbox,** Outbox, or Sent Items folders, Outlook moves the message to the Deleted Items folder, so it can fill up quickly.)

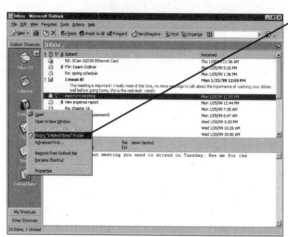

Choose the Empty "Deleted Items" Folder command to remove items from the selected folder.

# Calendar and Tasks

**You Can't Schedule a Meeting**

Outlook can be a marvelous tool for scheduling meetings, but scheduling can be a challenge when people are busy. Nevertheless, there are some things you can do to make it easier to schedule meetings.

### Use tentative appointments

Perhaps the easiest thing to do is tell Outlook that the **appointments** you schedule are **tentative appointments.** This way, the appointment time-slots you set aside don't fall into the **busy time** category, and Outlook can use them to schedule meetings. To indicate that an appointment is tentative, double-click the appointment to display the Appointment dialog box.

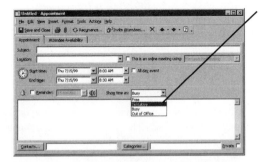

Select Tentative in the Show Time As list box to designate the appointment as tentative.

---

 **Leave free time in your schedule**

If you leave free time in your schedule—and everybody you work with does the same—you'll find it much easier to schedule meetings. You can even create a tentative appointment, perhaps called "meetings," and use it as an empty slot into which to insert real meetings.

---

 **Schedule shorter meetings**

What Outlook looks for when it schedules a meeting is a block of free time that is available to every meeting attendee. For this reason, it's easier to schedule half-hour meetings than to schedule one-hour meetings or two-hour meetings. There are many more half-hour slots in a day than there are one-hour or two-hour slots, after all.

ou Want Your Calendar and Task List to Be Private

As you may know, if you are on a network, almost everyone who uses Outlook can retrieve your free and busy time information from your **Calendar.** You may wonder, then, how private or public your schedule and **Tasks** list are. Unfortunately, I can't give you specific information about how private your schedule and Tasks list are, but I can give you some ideas for gaining a bit more privacy on the **network.**

*continues*

## You Want Your Calendar and Task List to Be Private *(continued)*

### Ask your administrator about delegate access permissions

You or the network administrator set what are called **delegate access** permissions to your schedule. Delegate access permissions determine who can view your Outlook information and whether they can change it. The default setting, by the way, is for other **users** to be able to see only when you're busy and when you're not. It's possible, however, for people to see much more detail. It all depends on the delegate access permissions. To view the delegate access permissions for a folder, right-click the folder in the Outlook Bar and choose the shortcut menu's Properties command. Then click the Permissions tab. If you have permission from your administrator to do so, you may be able to edit the delegate access permissions here for the folder you selected.

One more thing: If people can view your daily or weekly Calendar, they can see appointment and Tasks list descriptions as well. You can, however, create private appointment and task descriptions.

**SEE ALSO    Private Appointments and Tasks**

# Quick Reference

Any time you explore a new
program, you're bound to
see features and tools you
can't identify. To be sure
you can identify the
commands and toolbar
buttons you see in
Microsoft Outlook 2000, this
Quick Reference
describes these items in
systematic detail.

# Outlook Inbox Menu Commands

## File Menu

**New**  Displays the New submenu of items you can create.

**Mail Message**  Opens a new Message form.

**Post In This Folder**  Displays the Post form so you can place a post (or a file) in a folder.

**Folder...**  Lets you create a new folder.

**Outlook Bar Shortcut...**  Lets you add a folder icon to the Outlook Bar.

**Appointment**  Opens a new Appointment form.

**Meeting Request**  Opens a new Meeting Request form.

**Contact**  Opens a new Contact form.

**Distribution List**  Opens a new Distribution List form.

**Task**  Opens a new Task form.

**Task Request**  Opens a new Task Request form.

**Journal Entry**  Opens a new Journal Entry form.

**Note**  Opens a new Note.

**Office Document**  Opens a new Microsoft Office document.

**Choose Form...**  Opens a custom Outlook form.

**Personal Folders File (.pst)...**  Opens the Create Personal Folders dialog box.

**Open**  Opens the selected folder so you can see its contents or the selected message so you can read it.

**Selected Items**  Opens a message, task, or other item.

**Other User's Folder...**  Opens a Personal Folder from another person on the network.

**Personal Folders File (.pst)...**  Opens a Personal folder.

**Close All Items**  Closes all open Outlook items, including items minimized to the Taskbar.

| | |
|---|---|
| Save **A**s... | Saves the selected message in a different folder. |
| Save **Attachme**nts | Saves any attachments to the selected message in a different folder. |
| **F**older | Displays the Folder submenu. |

**N**ew Folder... Creates a new subfolder in the selected folder.

**S**end Link To This Folder Creates a new mail message with a hyperlink to the selected folder.

| | |
|---|---|
| Mo**v**e... | Moves the selected folder or message to a different location. |
| **C**opy... | Copies the selected folder or message to a different location. |

Cop**y** Folder Design... Copies the permissions, rules, description, forms, and views of the open folder.

| | |
|---|---|
| **D**elete | Deletes the selected message or folder. |
| **R**ename... | Renames the selected folder. |

Add To Public Folder Favori**t**es Adds the selected folder to the Favorites subfolder of Public Folders.

Remove From Public Folder Favori**t**es Removes the selected folder from the Favorites subfolder of Public Folders.

Proper**t**ies For Lets you view or change the properties of the selected message or folder.

| | |
|---|---|
| S**h**are | Displays the Share submenu. |
| **C**alendar | Allows you to share your Calendar with others across the Internet. |
| **T**asks | Allows you to share your Tasks folder with others. |
| C**o**ntacts | Allows you to share your Contacts folder with others. |
| T**h**is Folder | Allows you to share the currently selected folder with others. |
| Impor**t** And Export... | Starts the Import And Export Wizard. |

*continues*

## File Menu *(continued)*

| | |
|---|---|
| **Archive...** | Displays the Archive dialog box, enabling you to create Archiv files. |
| **Page Setup** | Displays the Page Setup submenu. |

| | |
|---|---|
| **Table Style** | Opens the Page Setup: Table Style dialog box to let you set table style printing options for printing messages. |
| **Memo Style** | Opens the Page Setup: Memo Style dialog box to let you set memo style printing options for printing messages. |

**Define Print Styles...** Opens the Define Print Styles dialog box.

| | |
|---|---|
| **Print Preview** | Displays a window that shows how printed messages look. |
| **Print...** | Prints the selected message. |
| **Work Offline** | Disconnects you if you are currently working online. |
| **Exit** | Stops the Outlook client program. |
| **Exit And Log Off** | Stops the Outlook client program and any other workgroup programs. |

## Edit Menu

| | |
|---|---|
| **Undo** | Reverses, or undoes, the last action. |
| **Cut** | Moves the current folder or item to the Clipboard. |
| **Copy** | Moves a copy of the current folder or item to the Clipboard. |
| **Paste** | Copies the Clipboard contents to the current folder. |
| **Clear** | Deletes the selected item(s). |
| **Select All** | Selects all the messages in the open folder. |
| **Delete** | Deletes the selected item(s). |
| **Move To Folder...** | Moves the selected item(s) to the folder you select. |
| **Copy To Folder...** | Copies the selected item(s) to the folder you select. |
| **Mark As Read** | Marks the selected message as one you've already read. |
| **Mark As Unread** | Marks the selected message as one you haven't yet read. |

| | |
|---|---|
| **Mark All As Read** | Marks all of the messages in the open folder as ones you've read. |
| **Categories...** | Lets you assign the selected item(s) to a category. |

## View Menu

| | |
|---|---|
| **Current View** | Displays the Current View submenu. |

**Messages**    Displays all messages.

**Messages With AutoPreview**  Displays a short preview of unread messages.

**By Follow Up Flag**  Groups messages by follow-up flag.

**Last Seven Days**  Lists only messages from the past week.

**Flagged For Next Seven Days**  Lists only messages that were flagged for the next week.

**By Conversation Topic**  Groups messages by conversation topic.

**By Sender**    Groups messages by sender.

**Unread Messages**  Lists unread messages only.

**Sent To**    Lists the time messages were sent and the names of the message recipients.

**Message Timeline**  Displays messages along a timeline.

**Customize Current View File...**  Displays the View Summary dialog box so you can edit a view.

**Define Views...**    Lets you create your own view.

**Format Columns...**  Displays the Format Columns dialog box, which allows you to define how flags and other items are viewed.

| | |
|---|---|
| **Go To** | Displays the Go To submenu. |

**Folder**    Moves to a folder elsewhere in Outlook or on your computer.

**Outlook Today**    Opens a window that lists Outlook items that need addressing.

*continues*

## View Menu *(continued)*

| | |
|---|---|
| **Inbox** | Displays your Inbox. |
| **Drafts** | Displays your Drafts folder. |
| **Calendar** | Displays your Calendar. |
| **Contacts** | Displays your Contacts folder. |
| **Tasks** | Displays your Tasks folder. |
| **News** | Opens Outlook Express News. |
| **Web Browser** | Starts your default web browser. |
| **Internet Call** | Displays the Internet Call submenu. |

**From Address Book...** Displays a dialog box that allows you to place a NetMeeting call to a person in an Address Book List.

**Internet Call** Starts Microsoft NetMeeting.

| | |
|---|---|
| **Outlook Bar** | Displays or hides the Outlook Bar of items and folders. |
| **Folder List** | Displays or hides the Folder List from the Outlook program window. (Outlook marks the command with a check mark when the Folder List is present.) |
| **Preview Pane** | Toggles the Preview pane on and off. |
| **AutoPreview** | Displays a short preview of each message. |
| **Expand/Collapse Groups** | Displays a submenu of commands for expanding and collapsing groups if the view uses groups. |
| **Toolbars** | Displays the Toolbars submenu. |

| | |
|---|---|
| **Standard** | Displays or hides the Standard toolbar. |
| **Advanced** | Display or hides the Advanced toolbar. |
| **Remote** | Displays or hides the Remote Mail toolbar. |
| **Web** | Displays or hides the Web toolbar. |
| **Customize...** | Displays a dialog box for rearranging the buttons on the toolbars. |

| | |
|---|---|
| **Status Bar** | Displays or hides the Outlook program window's status bar. (Outlook marks the command with a check mark when the status bar is present.) |

## Favorites Menu

**Add to Favorites...**     Adds currently selected item to your Favorites folder.

**Open Favorites...**     Opens your Favorites folder.

## Tools Menu

**Send**     Sends outgoing e-mail messages.

**Send/Receive**     Lets you choose the services to check for new e-mail.

**Synchronize**     Displays the Synchronize submenu for synchronizing Exchange folders.

      **All Folders**     Updates all your offline folders so they match the server folders that Outlook uses for the actual delivery and storage of real messages.

      **This Folder**     Updates the selected offline folder so it matches its server folder.

      **Offline Folder Settings**     Displays the folder settings for any offline folders you have.

      **Download Address Book**     Grabs the address lists from the Exchange server's Address Book, and stores them in the Address Book on your hard disk.

**Remote Mail**     Displays the Remote Mail submenu.

      **Connect...**     Dials your computer from a remote location so you can download message headers.

      **Disconnect**     Ends the dial-up connection to your computer from a remote location.

      **Mark To Retrieve**     Marks the messages you want to download to your computer when you reconnect.

      **Mark To Retrieve A Copy**     Marks the messages you want to download to your computer while leaving a copy on the server.

      **Delete**     Removes messages both from your computer and from the server.

      **Unmark**     Changes the status of a message that you had previously marked to download.

*continues*

## Tools Menu *(continued)*

| | |
|---|---|
| **Unmark All** | Changes the status of all the messages that you had previously marked to download. |
| **Remote Tools** | Displays the Remote toolbar. |

| | |
|---|---|
| **Dial-Up Connection** | Displays a submenu you can use to change your dial-up settings. |
| **Synchronize Other Computer** | Displays the Synchronize Other Computer submenu. |

| | |
|---|---|
| **Save File** | Opens the Save Synchronization File dialog box. |
| **Open File** | Opens the Open Synchronization File dialog box. |

| | |
|---|---|
| **Address Book...** | Displays the Address Book. |
| **Find** | Lets you locate messages that match your description. |
| **Advanced Find...** | Opens the Find dialog box with many options for finding items. |
| **Organize** | Opens the Organize pane. |
| **Rules Wizard...** | Starts the Rules Wizard, a tool for monitoring and managing incoming messages and other items. |
| **Out Of Office Assistant...** | Starts the Out Of Office Assistant, a tool for automatically handling messages you receive when you are out of the office. |
| **Microsoft Fax Tools** | Displays a submenu of commands for working with faxes and setting fax options. |
| **Empty "Deleted Items" Folder** | Removes all the items from the Deleted Items folder. |
| **Recover Deleted Items...** | Allows you to recover messages deleted from the Exchange server. |
| **Forms** | Displays the Forms submenu. |

| | |
|---|---|
| **Choose Form...** | Allows you to choose the form you want to use for creating an Outlook item. |
| **Design A Form...** | Allows you to design a custom form for creating Outlook items. |

| | |
|---|---|
| **Macro** | Displays the Macro submenu. |
| **Accounts... / Services...** | Describes and lets you change the information services available to the Outlook client. |

| | |
|---|---|
| **Customize** | Opens a dialog box allowing you to customize toolbars and menus. |
| **Options...** | Displays a dialog box you can use to control how the Outlook client works. |

## Actions Menu

| | |
|---|---|
| **New Mail Message** | Displays the Message form so you can create a new message. |
| **New Fax Message** | Opens a dialog box you can use to create a new fax. |
| **New Mail Message Using** | Displays a submenu so you can choose how you want to compose the message. |
| **Flag For Follow Up...** | Lets you flag a message so you can follow through with it later. |
| **Find All** | Opens the Find All submenu. |
| | **Related Messages...** Finds message with similar content and characteristics. |
| | **Messages From Sender...** Finds other messages from the sender. |
| **Junk E-Mail** | Displays the Junk E-Mail submenu. |
| | **Add To Junk Senders List** Adds the sender of the selected message to your Junk Senders list. |
| | **Add To Adult Content Senders List** Adds the sender of the selected message to your Adult Content Senders list. |
| **Reply** | Displays the RE: (Reply) form so you can respond to a message by sending the sender a new message. |
| **Reply To All** | Displays the RE: (Reply) form so you can respond to a message by sending the sender and all of the other message recipients a new message. |
| **Forward** | Displays the FW: (Forward) form so you can forward a copy of a message to somebody else. |

## Help Menu

| | |
|---|---|
| **Microsoft Outlook Help** | Displays the Office Assistant. |
| **Show/Hide The Office Assistant** | Toggles the Office Assistant on or off. |

*continues*

Help Menu *(continued)*

| | |
|---|---|
| **Microsoft Fax Help Topics** | Displays the Microsoft Fax Help Topics dialog box. |
| **What's This?** | Adds a question mark to the pointer, and displays an explanatory pop-up message the next time you click any item. |
| **Office On The Web** | Displays a web site with useful information about Outlook. |
| **Detect And Repair** | Fixes any errors in the Outlook program. |
| **About Microsoft Outlook** | Displays the About Microsoft Outlook dialog box, and gives information about the available memory and system resources. |

# Outlook Inbox Toolbar Buttons

| | |
|---|---|
| New | Displays the Message form so you can create a new message, or displays a drop-down list of other new items you can create. |
| | Prints the selected message. |
| | Moves the selected folder or message to a different location. |
| | Deletes the selected message or folder. |
| Reply | Displays the RE: (Reply) form so you can respond to a message by sending the sender a new message. |
| Reply to All | Displays the RE: (Reply To All) form so you can respond to a message by sending the sender and all of the other message recipients a new message. |
| Forward | Displays the FW: (Forward) form so you can forward a copy of a message to somebody else. |
| Send/Receive | Sends outgoing messages, and retrieves incoming messages. |
| Find | Opens the Find pane so you can search for messages. |
| Organize | Opens the Organize pane so you can move messages or change views. |
| | Displays the Address Book. |
| | Type a name here to search for a contact. |

Starts the Office Assistant.

 Shows more toolbar buttons or allows you to customize the toolbar.

# Message Form Commands

## File Menu

| | |
|---|---|
| **New** | Displays a submenu of new items you can create. |
| | **Mail Message**  Opens a new Message form. |
| | **Appointment**  Opens a new Appointment form. |
| | **Meeting Request**  Opens a new Meeting Request form. |
| | **Contact**  Opens a new Contact form. |
| | **Distribution List**  Opens a new Distribution List form. |
| | **Task**  Opens a new Task form. |
| | **Task Request**  Opens a new Task Request form. |
| | **Journal Entry**  Opens a new Journal Entry form. |
| | **Note**  Opens a new Note. |
| | **Post In This Folder**  Displays the Post form so you can place a post (or a file) in a folder. |
| | **Office Document**  Opens a new Microsoft Office document. |
| | **Choose Form...**  Displays a list of templates you can use. |
| **Send** | Sends the message. |
| **Send Using** | Allows you to select the service you want to use for sending the message (Internet Only version). |
| **Save** | Saves the message in the selected folder. |
| **Save Stationery...** | Allows you to save an HTML message you create as stationery, which you can use for creating other messages. |
| **Save As...** | Saves the message in the specified location. |
| **Save Attachments...** | Displays a submenu of any attachments to the message. |

*continues*

## File Menu *(continued)*

| | |
|---|---|
| **D**elete | Deletes the message. |
| **M**ove To Folder... | Moves the message to a different location. |
| Cop**y** To Folder... | Copies the message to a different location. |
| Page Set**u**p | Displays the Page Setup submenu. |

**Memo Style**   Opens the Page Setup: Memo Style dialog box to let you set memo style printing options for printing the message.

**Define Print Styles...** Opens the Define Print Styles dialog box.

| | |
|---|---|
| Print Pre**v**iew | Displays a window that shows how the printed message will look. |
| **P**rint... | Prints the message. |
| Prope**r**ties | Displays and lets you change the properties of the message. |
| **C**lose | Closes the Message form window. |

## **E**dit Menu

| | |
|---|---|
| **U**ndo | Reverses, or undoes, the last change to the message. |
| **R**edo | Restores the last change you reversed when you chose the Undo command. |
| Cu**t** | Moves the current message selection to the Clipboard. |
| **C**opy | Moves a copy of the current message selection to the Clipboard. |
| **P**aste | Copies the Clipboard contents to the message. |
| Paste **S**pecial... | Inserts the Clipboard contents or some portion of the Clipboard contents in the message. |
| Cle**a**r | Deletes selected message text. |
| Select A**l**l | Selects the entire message. |
| Mark As U**n**read | Marks the message as unread in the information viewer. |
| **E**dit Message | Allows you to edit the text of a message you receive. |
| **F**ind... | Looks for text that matches a specific description. |

**Find Ne<u>x</u>t**    Looks for the next instance of text that matches a specific description.

**<u>O</u>bject**    Displays a submenu of commands relating to the selected object.

## <u>V</u>iew Menu

**Pre<u>v</u>ious**    Displays the Previous submenu.

    **<u>I</u>tem**    Displays the previous message in the current folder.

    **<u>U</u>nread Item**    Displays the previous unread message in the current folder.

    **Item In <u>C</u>onversation Topic**    Displays the previous item in the current folder in the same conversation topic as the selected message.

    **Item From <u>S</u>ender**    Displays the previous item in the folder from the same sender as the sender of the selected message.

    **Hi<u>g</u>h Importance Item**    Displays the previous high-importance item in the current folder.

    **<u>F</u>lagged Message**    Displays the previous flagged message in the current folder.

    **Fi<u>r</u>st Item In Folder**    Displays the first item in the current folder.

**Ne<u>x</u>t**    Displays the Next submenu.

    **<u>I</u>tem**    Displays the next message in the current folder.

    **<u>U</u>nread Item**    Displays the next unread message in the current folder.

    **Item In <u>C</u>onversation Topic**    Displays the next item in the current folder in the same conversation topic as the selected message.

    **Item From <u>S</u>ender**    Displays the next item in the folder from the same sender as the sender of the selected message.

    **Hi<u>g</u>h Importance Item**    Displays the next high-importance item in the current folder.

*continues*

## View Menu *(continued)*

| | |
|---|---|
| | **Flagged Message**   Displays the next flagged message in the current folder. |
| | **Last Item In Folder**   Displays the last item in the current folder. |
| **Fonts** | Allows you to specify which font you want to use for reading messages you receive. |
| **Encoding** | Allows you to specify which country's character set you want to use to display a message. |
| **Message Header** | Toggles between the full message header and the short message header. |
| **From Field** | Displays or hides the From box in the Message form. (Outlook marks the command with a check mark when the From box is present.) |
| **Bcc Field** | Displays or hides the Bcc, or blind carbon copy, box in the Message form. (Outlook marks the command with a check mark when the Bcc box is present.) |
| **Options...** | Lets you set tracking, delivery, and status options for the message. |
| **Toolbars** | Displays the Toolbars submenu. |

| | | |
|---|---|---|
| | **Standard** | Displays or hides the Message form's Standard toolbar. (Outlook marks the command with a check mark when the Standard toolbar is present.) |
| | **Formatting** | Displays or hides the Message form's Formatting toolbar. (Outlook marks the command with a check mark when the Formatting toolbar is present.) |
| | **Clipboard** | Displays or hides the Message form's Clipboard toolbar. (Outlook marks the command with a check mark when the Clipboard toolbar is present.) |
| | **Customize...** | Displays a dialog box for rearranging the buttons on the toolbars. |

## Insert Menu

| | |
|---|---|
| **File...** | Inserts a file in your message. |
| **Item...** | Inserts a message (from an Outlook folder) in your message. |

| | |
|---|---|
| **O**bject... | Inserts an object such as a drawing or a piece of WordArt text art in a message (Rich Text only). |
| **S**ignature | Displays a submenu for choosing a signature to insert in your message. |
| **Horizontal Line** | Draws a horizontal line across an HTML message. |
| **P**icture... | Opens the Picture dialog box so you can insert art in an HTML message. |
| **H**yperlink... | Opens a dialog box so you can type a URL address in an HTML message. |
| **R**emove Hyperlink | Turns a hyperlink in an HTML message into normal text. |

## Format Menu

| | | |
|---|---|---|
| **Style** | Opens a submenu for choosing a style for text in an HTML message. | |
| **Font**... | Changes the font of the selected characters. | |
| **P**aragraph... | Changes the alignment of the selected paragraphs, and adds or removes bullets. | |
| **Background** | Opens the Background submenu. | |
| | **P**icture... | Opens the Picture dialog box so you can choose a picture as the background of an HTML message. |
| | **C**olor | Lets you choose a color for the background of an HTML message. |
| **E**ncoding | Allows you to specify the alphabet you want to use for creating the message. | |
| **Plain Text** | Formats an HTML message as plain text. | |
| **HTML** | Formats a message as an HTML file, which allows you to add advanced formatting and images to your message. | |
| **R**ich Text | Formats a message as rich text, which allows you to add character and paragraph formatting. | |
| **Send Pictures From The Internet** | Formats an HTML message so that JPEG or GIF images you include are sent along with the message. | |

## Tools Menu

| | |
|---|---|
| **Spelling...** | Checks the spelling of the words you used in your message. |
| **Check Names** | Verifies that you've correctly spelled the recipient names. |
| **Address Book...** | Displays the Address Book. |
| **Fax Addressing Wizard...** | Starts the Fax Addressing Wizard, which helps you address faxes. |
| **Forms** | Opens the Message [Design] dialog box so you can design a custom form. |

**Choose Form...** Allows you to choose which form you want to use for creating the message.

**Design This Form** Opens the Untitled Message Design form which you can use to create a new message form.

**Design A Form...** Opens a dialog box that lets you select an existing form from which you can create a new form.

**Publish Form** Allows you to save the form you create.

**Publish Form As...** Opens a dialog box that allows you to save the form you create under the name you specify.

**Script Debugger** Runs the Script Debugger, which helps you fix errors in the scripts you create for custom forms.

| | |
|---|---|
| **Macro** | Displays the Macro submenu you can use to create or run macros. |
| **Customize...** | Displays a dialog box for rearranging the buttons on the toolbars. |

## Actions Menu

| | |
|---|---|
| **New Mail Message** | Displays the Message form so you can create a new message. |
| **New Fax Message** | Starts a wizard that guides you through the process of creating a fax. |
| **Flag For Follow Up** | Opens a dialog box so you can flag the form. |

| | |
|---|---|
| **Fi̲nd All** | Displays the Find All submenu. |
| | **R̲elated Messages...** Finds all other messages that have the same conversation topic as the currently open message. |
| | **M̲essages From Sender...** Finds all messages received from the sender of the displayed message. |
| **R̲eply** | Displays the RE: (Reply) form so you can respond to a message by sending the sender a new message. |
| **Reply To A̲ll** | Displays the RE: (Reply) form so you can respond to a message by sending the sender and all of the other message recipients a new message. |
| **For̲ward** | Displays the FW: (Forward) form so you can forward a copy of a message to somebody else. |
| **Recall T̲his Message...** | Attempts to retrieve a sent message before it is read by the recipient. |
| **Resend T̲his Message...** | Opens a copy of the message so you can send it again. |

## Help Menu

| | |
|---|---|
| **Microsoft Outlook H̲elp** | Displays the Office Assistant. |
| **Show/Hide The Office Assistant** | Toggles the Office Assistant on or off. |
| **Microsoft Fa̲x Help Topics** | Displays the Microsoft Fax Help Topics dialog box. |
| **What's T̲his?** | Adds a question mark to the pointer, and displays an explanatory pop-up message the next time you click any item. |
| **Office On The W̲eb** | Displays a web site with useful information about Outlook. |
| **Detect And R̲epair** | Fixes any errors in the Outlook program. |
| **A̲bout Microsoft Outlook** | Displays the About Microsoft Outlook dialog box, and gives information about the available memory and system resources. |

# Message Form Toolbar Buttons

| | |
|---|---|
|  | Sends the message. |
|  | Displays a list of message accounts you can use to send your message (Internet Only version). |

*continues*

## Message Form Toolbar Buttons *(continued)*

| | |
|---|---|
| | Saves the message in a specified folder using a specified name. |
| | Prints the message. |
| | Moves the current selection to the Clipboard. |
| | Moves a copy of the current selection to the Clipboard. |
| | Copies the Clipboard contents to the Message form. |
| | Inserts a signature. |
| | Inserts a file in your message. |
| | Opens the Select Names dialog box. |
| | Checks recipient names. |
| | Sets the message importance to "high." |
| | Sets the message importance to "low." |
| | Adds a flag to the message. |
| Options... | Opens the Message Options dialog box. |
| | Displays the Office Assistant. |

## Interested in what the Formatting toolbar buttons do?

I'm not going to describe what the Formatting tools do here. I already described them in the **Character Formatting** entry in this book.

# Item-Specific Menu Commands

## The Calendar Folder's Actions Menu

| | |
|---|---|
| **New Appointment** | Lets you schedule a new appointment. |
| **New All Day Event** | Lets you schedule a new event. |
| **New Meeting Request** | Displays a Message form you can use to invite people to a meeting. |
| **Plan A Meeting...** | Lets you plan and schedule a meeting. |
| **New Recurring Appointment** | Lets you schedule a new appointment that recurs regularly. |
| **New Recurring Meeting** | Lets you schedule a new meeting that recurs regularly. |
| **Add Or Remove Attendees** | Lets you change the attendee list for a meeting. |
| **Forward As iCalendar** | Forwards the selected appointment as an iCalendar attachment in a message. |
| **Forward** | Displays the FW: (Forward) form so you can forward information about an appointment, meeting, or event to somebody else. |

## The Contacts Folder's Actions Menu

| | |
|---|---|
| **New Contact** | Lets you add a new contact to your Contacts list. |
| **New Contact From Same Company** | Lets you add to your Contacts list a new contact from the same company as the selected contact. |
| **New Distribution List** | Opens a new Distribution List form. |
| **New Fax Message** | Starts a wizard that helps you create a fax. |
| **New Message To Contact** | Opens a new Message form so you can send the contact an e-mail message. |
| **New Letter To Contact** | Opens Microsoft Word and starts the Letter Wizard so you can write a letter to the contact. |
| **New Meeting Request To Contact** | Lets you set up a meeting with someone on your Contacts list. |
| **New Appointment With Contact** | Opens a new appointment form with the selected contact. |

*continues*

## The Contacts Folder's Actions Menu *(continued)*

| | |
|---|---|
| **New Task For Contact** | Opens a new Task form so that you can send the contact a task request. |
| **New Journal Entry For Contact** | Opens a new Journal entry for contact. |
| **Link** | Allows you to link a document or Outlook item to the selected contact. |
| **Call Contact** | Displays a submenu of commands for calling contacts. |
| **Call Using NetMeeting** | Opens NetMeeting and initiates a call with the contact. |
| **Flag For Follow Up...** | Flags a contact for follow up. |
| **Forward As vCard** | Forwards the selected contact item as a vCard attachment in a message. |

## The Tasks Folder's Actions Menu

| | |
|---|---|
| **New Task** | Lets you add a new task to your Tasks list. |
| **New Task Request** | Lets you send a message requesting a task be performed. |
| **Save Task Order** | Saves the order of the current Tasks list. |
| **Forward** | Lets you forward information about a task in an e-mail message. |

# A

access permissions .............. 40, 114, 164
actions ..................................................... 16
> See also rules and actions

Actions menu
> Calendar folder .............................. 183
> Contacts folder ......................... 183–84
> Inbox folder ................................... 173
> Message form ........................... 180–81
> Tasks folder ................................... 184

activities, defined ................................. 16
adaptability ..................................... 16–17
Address Book. *See also* Global Address List
> adding e-mail names ...................... 17
> defined ........................................ 4, 17
> distribution lists ........................ 42–43
> using to send e-mail ...................... 18

Address Cards view ......................... 34, 36
addresses. *See* Global Address List;
> Personal Address Book

administrator ....................................... 164
alarms. *See* reminders
aliases, e-mail ...................................... 44
aligning text ..................................... 18–19
anniversaries, adding to Calendar 29–30
announcements. *See* post messages
annual events
> adding to Calendar ................... 29–30
> categorizing ............................... 31–32
> setting reminders ............................ 30

applications. *See* programs
appointments. *See also* events; meetings
> adding to Calendar ............. 19–20, 31
> private ..................................... 114–15
> recurring ..................................... 119–20
> rescheduling ................................... 39
> setting reminders .............. 20, 121–22
> shortcut for entering ....................... 31
> tentative ........................... 146, 162–63

archives
> creating ...................................... 20–22
> retrieving .................................... 22–23

attaching
> certificates ..................................... 41
> files to e-mail messages ............. 78–79

attaching *(continued)*
> files to post messages .................... 112
> Outlook items to e-mail
> > messages .................................. 79–80
> Outlook items to post
> > messages ................................. 111–12

attachments, defined ........................... 20
audio conferences. *See* NetMeeting
AutoArchive feature ...................... 20–23
AutoCreate feature ............................... 23
AutoDial feature ............................ 23–24
automatic message delivery .............. 24
AutoPreview feature ...................... 24–25
AutoReply feature. *See* Out Of Office
> Assistant

# B

Bcc field ................................................ 25
birthdays, adding to Calendar ...... 29–30
blind carbon copies ............................. 25
bullets, in e-mail messages ................. 26
business cards, virtual ....................... 149
busy times, defined ........................ 26–27
buttons, toolbar, displaying names .... 33

# C

Calendar
> Actions menu ................................. 183
> adding anniversaries ................ 29–30
> adding annual events ............... 29–30
> adding appointments ............... 19–20
> adding birthdays ....................... 29–30
> adding events ........................... 31, 46
> adding holidays ............................. 30
> busy times .................................. 26–27
> changing view ..................... 28, 38–39
> customizing ..................................... 28
> Date Navigator ............. 27, 28, 38–39
> delegate access
> > permissions ............. 40, 114–15, 164
> displaying schedule ................. 38–39
> display options .......................... 28–29
> filtering items ................................. 51

Calendar *(continued)*
   free time ............................ 26–27, 163
   overview ...................................... 8–9, 27
   recurring appointments ......... 119–20
   rescheduling appointments .......... 39
   second time zone ..................... 126–27
   setting reminders ............. 20, 121–22
   sharing information ................. 62–63
   shortcut for entering events ......... 31
   troubleshooting ...................... 162–64
carbon copies ................................. 25, 37
categories
   for annual events ...................... 31–32
   assigning .................................... 31–32
   filtering messages by ..................... 68
   for notes ......................................... 97
   searching by ................................... 52
   for tasks ................................... 32, 145
certificate attachments ........................ 41
character formatting...................... 32–33
Check Names feature .......................... 33
clients
   Outlook as client .......................... 103
   vs. servers ..................................... 129
color-coding notes .............................. 97
columns, Inbox display ................. 107–8
   *See also* fields
composing
   e-mail messages ...................... 4–5, 78
   post messages ............................... 111
conferencing. *See* NetMeeting
Connection Wizard ............................. 34
Contacts folder
   Actions menu .......................... 183–84
   adding names ................... 34–35, 158
   Address Cards view ................. 34, 36
   changing view ................................ 35
   finding items ............................. 51–53
   looking up names .......................... 36
   overview .............................. 10–11, 34
   storing NetMeeting information ..... 90
   tracking contacts in Journal ......... 73
conversation threads
   and e-mail messages ................. 36–37
   and post messages ........................ 112
copying messages ....................... 25, 37
custom forms ...................................... 38

**D**

data compression ............................... 15.
Date Navigator ................... 27, 28, 38–3⁹
dates, selecting ............................... 38–3⁹
deferred delivery .............................. 3⁹
delegate access
   permissions .......... 40, 114–15, 16·
Deleted Items folder .............. 77, 81, 162
delivery, deferred .............................. 3⁹
delivery receipts ..................... 40–41, 16⁰
designing forms................................. 5⁸
dialing telephone numbers
   speed dialing .............................. 13⁵
   using AutoDial .......................... 23–24
digital ID ...................................... 41–42
directories. *See* folders
distribution lists
   creating ..................................... 42–43·
   overview ....................................... 42·
   using ............................................. 43·
Drafts folder ....................................... 44·

**E**

Edit menu (Inbox) ............................. 168·
Edit menu (Message form) ......... 176–77·
electronic business cards .................. 149·
electronic mail. *See* e-mail
e-mail. *See also* distribution lists;
   messages, e-mail
   adding names to Address Book ..... 17·
   aliases ............................................ 44·
   confirming message delivery ... 40–41·
   confirming message opening... 118–19·
   controlling amount ................. 160–61·
   defined ........................................... 44·
   deleting messages ................... 161–62·
   etiquette ......................................... 44·
   finding addresses ................... 156–59·
   forwarding messages ........ 58, 82, 161·
   and HTML ............................. 61, 139·
   junk mail messages ........... 75–76, 161·
   problems with .......................... 159–61·
   replying to messages ... 81–82, 123, 161·

e-mail *(continued)*
    troubleshooting ..................... 156–62
    using Address Book to send
        messages......................................... 18
e-mail names ........................................ 45
emptying folders ......................... 161–62
encryption ........................................... 45
etiquette
    e-mail .............................................. 44
    flames ............................................. 53
Eudora ................................................. 45
events
    adding to Calendar ......................... 46
    categorizing ............................... 31–32
    defined ........................................... 45
    recurring.................................... 29–30
    setting reminders ........................... 30
    viewing information ................. 46–47
Exchange server. *See* Microsoft Exchange
        server

**F**

Favorites folder ............................... 47–48
Favorites menu (Inbox) ..................... 171
faxes
    overview .......................................... 48
    sending ...................................... 48–49
    setting options .............................. 49
fields ................................................... 50
        *See also* columns
File menu (Inbox) ........................ 166–68
File menu (Message form) .......... 175–76
files. *See also* folders
    attaching to e-mail messages ... 78–79
    attaching to post messages........... 112
    compressing ................................. 153
    defined............................................. 50
filters
    categorizing items........................... 68
    for e-mail messages .......... 66–69, 161
    in Inbox folder ......................... 66–69
    overview ......................................... 51
    in Tasks list................................ 141–42
finding
    e-mail addresses ..................... 156–59

finding *(continued)*
    Outlook items ........................... 51–53
flagging messages ........................... 84–85
flames ................................................. 53
Folder Banner..................................... 54
Folder List .......................................... 55
folders. *See also* Calendar; Contacts folder;
        Inbox; Journal; notes; tasks
    Calendar folder ......................... 27–31
    creating ..................................... 53–54
    creating views ............. 55–56, 150–51
    defined ...................................... 53–54
    deleting messages..................... 161–62
    displaying list ................................. 55
    Drafts folder ................................... 44
    emptying................................... 161–62
    Favorites folder ......................... 47–48
    filtering folder items....................... 51
    folders within ............................... 139
    information viewer ................... 69–70
    My Documents folder .................... 89
    naming............................................ 54
    Net Folders feature ........................ 90
    offline ................................... 98, 123
    organizing ............................... 98–100
    Outlook overview ........................ 6–7
    personal ............................... 7, 109
    public ....................... 7, 111, 117
    synchronizing ......................... 140–41
    troubleshooting ..................... 161–62
    using views .................................... 56
    viewing hierarchy .......................... 55
    Web Folder icon ........................... 152
fonts ............................................ 56–57
Format menu (Message form) ......... 179
formatting
    e-mail message text ................. 32–33
    HTML in e-mail messages ..... 61, 139
    options for e-mail message ...... 86–87
forms. *See also* Message form
    custom .............................................. 38
    defined ........................................... 57
    designing ........................................ 58
forwarding
    e-mail messages ............... 58, 82, 161
    post messages ............................... 113
free time ...................................26–27, 163

## G

Global Address List ................ 42, 58, 157
    *See also* Address Book
Go menu (Inbox) ............................... 170
Group buttons .................................... 101
Group By box ....................................... 59
grouping. *See also* conversation threads
    e-mail messages ........................ 59–60
    post messages ................................ 112
    tasks .......................................... 59–60
group scheduling ................................ 60

## H

Help feature ........................................ 60
    *See also* Office Assistant
Help menu (Inbox) .................... 173–74
Help menu (Message form) ............. 181
holidays, adding to Calendar ............. 30
HTML ............................................ 61, 139
hyperlinks ...................................... 61–62

## I

iCalendar ......................................... 62–63
icons, toolbar, displaying names ........ 33
IMAP (Internet Message Access
    Protocol) .................................... 63
importance, message ..................... 63–64
Import And Export Wizard ......... 64–65
importing items and files ............. 64–65
Inbox
    column options.......................... 107–8
    defined ..................................... 6–7, 66
    deleting messages.......................... 161
    emptying...................................... 161
    menus ..................................... 166–74
    previewing messages ................ 24–25
    read vs. unread messages ............. 117
    received messages ..................... 80–81
    toolbar buttons ....................... 174–75
    using filters................................ 66–69

Inbox Assistant. *See* Rules Wizard
information services ............................ 6?
information viewer ........................ 69–7(
    *See also* panes
Insert menu (Message form) ...... 178–7?
installing Outlook Express ................. 9?
international date line ...................... 12(
Internet ........................................ 70, 15?
Internet Explorer ......................... 34, 7(
Internet Message Access Protocol
    (IMAP) ....................................... 6?
Internet Only version, Outlook .......... 7?
Internet service providers ........... 2–3, 7?
intranets .............................................. 7?
items. *See also* appointments; Contacts
    folder; Journal; meetings; mes-
    sages, e-mail; notes; tasks
    creating using AutoCreate ....... 23–24
    defined ......................................... 7?
    sorting...................................... 133–34
item-specific menus ..................... 183–84
    *See also* Actions menu

## J

Journal
    automatic recordkeeping ......... 73–7?
    manual recordkeeping ................... 75
    overview .............................. 12–13, 72
    tracking activities...................... 73–75
    uses for....................................... 73–74
junk e-mail ............................. 75–76, 16?

## K

kilobits .................................................. 76
kilobytes ............................................... 76

## L

laptop computers ................................. 76

# M

mail. *See* messages, e-mail
Mailbox ......................................... 77
> *See also* Inbox
Mail folders ................................. 77
mail merge ................................. 153
marking e-mail messages ................. 117
Meeting Planner. *See* meetings
meetings
> adding to schedule ..................... 31
> group scheduling ............ 60, 109–10
> keeping short ......................... 163
> NetMeeting ........................... 90–91
> and permissions ..................... 114–15
> Plan A Meeting Wizard ......... 109–10
> shortcut for entering ............... 31
menus
> item-specific (*See* actions)
> personalizing ......................... 156
message expiration ....................... 84
message flag ........................... 84–85
Message form
> adding hyperlinks ................. 61–62
> aligning text in ..................... 18–19
> bullets in messages ............... 26
> formatting messages ............. 32–33
> menu commands ................. 175–81
> message body ....................... 83
> message header ..................... 87
> overview ........................... 4–5, 85
> sensitivity level ................. 128–29
> toolbar buttons ................. 181–82
> using fonts ....................... 56–57
> writing messages ............... 4–5, 78
messages, e-mail. *See also* Message form;
> post messages
> adding hyperlinks ............... 61–62
> assigning priority ............... 63–64
> attaching files ................. 78–79
> attaching Outlook items ......... 79–80
> automatic delivery ............... 24
> automatic replies ............... 104–6
> bullets in ......................... 26
> composing ....................... 4–5, 78

messages *(continued)*
> confirming delivery ............. 40–41
> confirming opening ............. 118–19
> conversation threads ........... 36–37
> deferred delivery ............... 39
> defined ........................... 78
> delegate access
> > permissions ............... 40, 114–15
> deleting ..................... 81, 161–62
> filtering ................. 66–69, 161
> finding ..................... 51–53
> flagging ................... 84–85
> flames ....................... 53
> format options ............. 86–87
> formatting messages ......... 32–33
> forwarding ............. 58, 82, 161
> grouping ................. 59–60
> HTML formatting ............. 61
> HTML stationery ............. 139
> identifying subject ......... 140
> incoming ................. 6–7
> junk mail ............. 75–76, 161
> marking ................. 117
> message body ............. 83
> message header ........... 87
> previewing ............. 24–25
> printing ............... 83
> reading ........... 6–7, 80–81
> read vs. unread ......... 117
> receiving ............. 6–7
> replying automatically ....... 104–6
> replying to ......... 81–82, 123, 161
> sealing ............. 41–42, 126
> sending ............. 4–5, 80
> sending copies ......... 25, 37
> sensitivity level ......... 128–29
> setting options ......... 88
> sorting ............. 133–34
> spell checking ......... 136–37
> ungrouping ......... 59
> using Address Book to send ... 18
Microsoft Exchange server
> checking status of ......... 159
> defined ............. 2, 47, 103
> delivery receipts ......... 40–41, 160

Microsoft Exchange server *(continued)*
    information services ...................... 69
    read receipts ................... 118–19, 160
Microsoft Fax ........................... 48–49
Microsoft Schedule+ .......................... 27
Microsoft Word, as e-mail
    editor ................................. 152–53
MIME ...................................... 89
monthly calendar. *See* Date Navigator
moving notes ........................................ 96
My Documents folder ......................... 89

## N

names
    adding to Address Book ................ 17
    in Contact list.............................. 158
    e-mail names ..................................... 45
    finding addresses ................... 156–59
    in Global Address List ...... 42, 58, 157
    verifying using Check Names ........ 33
Net Folders feature .............................. 90
netiquette ............................................. 44
NetMeeting...................................... 90–91
network administrator ...................... 164
networks. *See also* Internet; Microsoft
    Exchange server
    defined ............................... 91
    intranets ............................ 72
    and Outlook ................................... 2–3
newsgroups
    posting messages to ....................... 95
    previewing in Outlook Express ..... 92
    reading messages .......................... 93
    subscribing to.............................. 92
    unsubscribing from ....................... 92
newsreaders, defined .......................... 91
    *See also* Outlook Express
notebooks. *See* laptop computers
notes
    categorizing ..................................... 97
    coloring ............................. 97
    customizing..................................... 96
    deleting ............................. 97
    keeping track of ........................... 97

notes *(continued)*
    moving.............................................. 9‹
    overview ............................. 12–13, 9‹
    printing............................................. 9‹
    resizing............................................. 9‹
    viewing............................................. 9‹
    writing ............................................. 9
numbers. *See* phone numbers

## O

Office Assistant ................................. 9‹
offline folders ....................... 98, 123, 14‹
online Help ............................................ 6‹
online meetings. *See* NetMeeting
online services. *See* Internet service
    providers
organization, defined ......................... 9‹
Organize pane ...................... 98–100, 16‹
Outbox folder...................................... 7‹
Outlook
    importing items and files ......... 64–6‹
    Internet Only version ..................... 7‹
    navigating ...................................... 10‹
    overview ......................................... 2–‹
    Startup Wizard ...................... 137–3‹
Outlook Bar
    accessing folders ....................... 101–‹
    customizing................................... 10‹
    navigating Outlook ...................... 10‹
    overview ......................................... 10‹
    when to use ................................... 10‹
Outlook client ............................. 2, 10‹
Outlook Express
    installing ............................. 9‹
    and multipart message
      attachments ................................. 9‹
    vs. Outlook ................................... 10‹
    posting messages with
      attachments ................................. 9‹
    posting simple messages ............... 9‹
    previewing newsgroups................. 9‹
    reading attachments ................ 93–9‹
    reading messages .......................... 9‹
    starting................................. 9‹

Outlook Express *(continued)*
stopping large message
downloads ..................................... 94
subscribing to newsgroups ............ 92
unsubscribing from newsgroups .. 92
Outlook folders .................................... 103
*See also* folders
Outlook Today .............................. 103–4
Out Of Office Assistant
creating standard response .......... 104
defined ............................................. 104
list of actions .................................. 106
rules and actions ....................... 105–6
using ........................................... 104–6

## P

panes ............................................... 107–8
permissions ......................................... 108
*See also* delegate access permissions
Personal Address Book. *See also* Address
Book
adding names ................................... 17
distribution lists ......................... 42–43
overview ..................................... 108–9
using to send e-mail ....................... 18
personal folders ............................. 7, 109
Personal Menus feature ..................... 156
phone numbers
dialing ......................................... 23–24
speed dialing ................................. 135
tracking calls .................................... 74
Plan A Meeting Wizard ............... 109–10
Pocket Outlook .................................... 110
posting post messages ................. 111–12
post messages
attaching files ............................... 112
attaching Outlook items ........ 111–12
and conversation threads ............. 112
forwarding .................................... 113
grouping ......................................... 112
overview ......................................... 110
posting to newsgroups ................... 95
posting to public folders ........ 111–12
printing .......................................... 113

post messages *(continued)*
public folders for .............. 7, 111, 117
reading ............................................ 112
replying to ..................................... 113
writing ............................................ 111
previewing incoming messages .... 24–25
Preview pane ....................................... 114
printing
e-mail messages ............................... 83
notes.................................................. 97
post messages ............................... 113
prioritizing tasks ................................ 145
priority level, e-mail ...................... 63–64
privacy
delegate access
permissions ................... 114–15, 164
keeping appointments
private ..................................... 114–15
maintaining .................................... 164
private appointments .................. 114–15
private folders. *See* personal folders
Private Sensitivity level ...................... 129
private tasks ................................... 114–15
profiles .................................. 116, 137–38
programs, defined .............................. 116
program windows, defined .............. 116
project management .............. 32, 145–46
protocols
MIME ............................................... 89
SMTP ............................................... 133
public folders ......................... 7, 111, 117

## R

reading
e-mail messages ......................... 80–81
messages in public folders ........... 112
newsgroup messages ...................... 93
read receipts ......................... 118–19, 160
receipts
delivery receipts ............... 40–41, 160
read receipts ................... 118–19, 160
recipients, defined .............................. 119
recordkeeping. *See* Journal
recurring appointments .............. 119–20

recurring events
    adding to Calendar ................... 29–30
    appointments .......................... 119–20
    categorizing .............................. 31–32
    setting reminders ......................... 30
recurring tasks ............................. 120–21
registered mail. *See* delivery receipts;
    read receipts
reminders .......................... 20, 30, 121–22
Remote Mail feature .................... 122–23
replying
    to e-mail messages .... 81–82, 123, 161
    to post messages ........................... 113
rescheduling appointments ............... 39
resizing notes ......................................... 96
Rich Text Format (RTF) files ............. 56
Rolodex. *See* Address Book; Address
    Cards view
RTF files ................................................ 56
rules and actions
    applying rules .............................. 125
    creating rules ........................... 123–25
    customizing rules ........................ 125
    defined ........................................ 123
Rules Wizard ................................ 123–25

**S**

Schedule+ ............................................. 27
scheduling. *See also* Calendar
    and access permissions ..... 40, 114–15
    displaying schedule .................. 38–39
    free time ............................ 26–27, 163
sealed messages ...................... 41–42, 126
second time zone ......................... 126–27
security. *See also* privacy
    digital ID .................................... 41–42
    encryption ...................................... 45
    overview ....................................... 127
security zones ...................................... 128
sender, defined .................................... 128
sending
    e-mail ............................... 4–5, 24, 80
    faxes ........................................... 48–49
sensitivity, message ...................... 128–29

Sent Items folder ................................... 7
server extensions ......................... 129–3
servers ............................................. 2, 12
    *See also* Microsoft Exchange server
shortcut icons .................................... 13
signatures
    digital ......................................... 41–4
    for e-mail messages ................. 130–3
smileys ................................................ 13
SMTP (simple mail transport
    protocol) ..................................... 13
sorting ............................................. 133–3
spam .................................................... 13
Speed Dial feature ............................. 13
spelling checker ............................. 136–3
Start menu .............................................. 5
Startup Wizard ............................. 137–3
stationery ............................................ 13
status bar ............................................ 13
subfolders ........................................... 13
subjects, in message header ............. 14
subscribing to newsgroups ................. 9
synchronizing folders .................. 140–4

**T**

TaskPad .......................................... 9, 14
tasks
    accepting ........................................ 14
    Actions menu ................................ 18
    adding to Tasks list ...................... 14
    assigning to others ....................... 14
    categorizing ........................... 32, 14
    declining ........................................ 14
    defined .......................................... 14
    filtering .................................... 141–4
    finding ....................................... 51–5
    grouping ............................... 32, 59–6
    prioritizing .................................... 14
    private ...................................... 114–1
    reassigning .................................... 14
    recurring ................................... 120–2
    reporting status ............................ 14
    setting reminders ................... 121–2
    tracking status .............................. 14

tasks *(continued)*
    ungrouping ........................................ 59
    viewing Tasks list ......................... 143
telephone numbers
    dialing ................................... 23–24
    speed dialing .................................... 135
    tracking calls .................................... 74
tentative appointments ....... 146, 162–63
text
    aligning ........................................ 18–19
    changing fonts ........................... 56–57
    filtering messages by ...................... 68
    formatting e-mail messages ..... 32–33
threads. *See* conversation threads
time zone, second ......................... 126–27
to-do lists ............................................ 146
    *See also* tasks
toolbars
    displaying button names ................ 33
    Inbox tools ............................... 174–75
    Message form ........................... 181–82
    overview ......................................... 147
Tools menu (Inbox) .................... 171–73
Tools menu (Message form) ............. 180
ToolTips ................................................ 33
tracking. *See* Journal
troubleshooting
    Calendar .................................. 162–64
    e-mail ...................................... 156–62
    folder use ................................. 161–62

**U**

undoing actions ................................... 147
ungrouping
    messages ........................................... 59
    tasks ................................................. 59
unread messages ................................. 117
unsubscribing from newsgroups ........ 92
URLs ..................................................... 148
users, defined ..................................... 148
Uuencode ...................................... 148–49

**V**

vCard ................................................... 149
VeriSign service .................................... 41
video conferences. *See* NetMeeting
View menu (Inbox) ..................... 169–70
View menu (Message form) ....... 177–78
views
    Calendar ........................ 28–29, 38–39
    creating ........................ 55–56, 150–51
    modifying ....................................... 150
    switching ........................................ 150
virtual business cards ........................ 149
voting buttons .................................... 151

**W**

Web browsers ...................................... 152
Web Folder icon .................................. 152
Web pages ........................................... 152
Windows CE ........................................ 110
wizards
    Connection Wizard ......................... 34
    Import And Export Wizard ..... 64–65
    Plan A Meeting Wizard .......... 109–10
    Rules Wizard ........................... 123–25
    Startup Wizard ....................... 137–38
Word. *See* Microsoft Word
World Wide Web .................................. 153
writing
    e-mail messages ...................... 4–5, 78
    post messages ................................. 111

**Z**

ZIP files ............................................... 153

The manuscript for this book was prepared and submitted to Microsoft Press in electronic form. Text files were prepared using Microsoft Word 97. Pages were composed by Stephen L. Nelson, Inc., using PageMaker 6.5 for Windows, with text in Minion and display type in Univers. Composed pages were delivered to the printer as electronic prepress files.

**Cover Designer**
Tim Girvin Design, Inc.

**Layout**
Jeff Adell

**Project Editor**
Paula Thurman

**Copy Editor**
Rebecca Whitney

**Writers**
Jason Gerend and Steve Nelson

**Technical Editor**
Brian Milbrath

**Indexer**
Julie Kawabata

*Printed on recycled paper stock.*

# See clearly—
# *now!*

**H**ere's the remarkable, *visual* way to quickly find answers about the powerfully integrated features of the Microsoft® Office 2000 applications. Microsoft Press AT A GLANCE books let you focus on particular tasks and show you, with clear, numbered steps, the easiest way to get them done right now. Put Office 2000 to work today, with AT A GLANCE learning solutions, made by Microsoft.

- MICROSOFT OFFICE 2000 PROFESSIONAL AT A GLANCE
- MICROSOFT WORD 2000 AT A GLANCE
- MICROSOFT EXCEL 2000 AT A GLANCE
- MICROSOFT POWERPOINT® 2000 AT A GLANCE
- MICROSOFT ACCESS 2000 AT A GLANCE
- MICROSOFT FRONTPAGE® 2000 AT A GLANCE
- MICROSOFT PUBLISHER 2000 AT A GLANCE
- MICROSOFT OFFICE 2000 SMALL BUSINESS AT A GLANCE
- MICROSOFT PHOTODRAW® 2000 AT A GLANCE
- MICROSOFT INTERNET EXPLORER 5 AT A GLANCE
- MICROSOFT OUTLOOK® 2000 AT A GLANCE

mspress.microsoft.com

# Stay in the *running* for maximum productivity.

These are *the* answer books for business users of Microsoft® Office 2000. They are packed with everything from quick, clear instructions for new users to comprehensive answers for power users—the authoritative reference to keep by your computer and use every day. THE RUNNING SERIES—learning solutions made by Microsoft.

- RUNNING MICROSOFT 2000 EXCEL 2000
- RUNNING MICROSOFT OFFICE 2000 PREMIUM
- RUNNING MICROSOFT OFFICE 2000 PROFESSIONAL
- RUNNING MICROSOFT OFFICE 2000 SMALL BUSINESS
- RUNNING MICROSOFT WORD 2000
- RUNNING MICROSOFT POWERPOINT® 2000
- RUNNING MICROSOFT ACCESS 2000
- RUNNING MICROSOFT INTERNET EXPLORER 5
- RUNNING MICROSOFT FRONTPAGE® 2000
- RUNNING MICROSOFT OUTLOOK® 2000

Microsoft Press® products are available worldwide wherever quality computer books are sold. For more information, contact your book or computer retailer, software reseller, or local Microsoft Sales Office, or visit our Web site at mspress.microsoft.com. To locate your nearest source for Microsoft Press products, or to order directly, call 1-800-MSPRESS in the U.S. (in Canada, call 1-800-268-2222).

Prices and availability dates are subject to change.

mspress.microsoft.com